# REBUILDING

# SHAKESPEARE'S

# GLOBE

# REBUILDING SHAKESPEARE'S GLOBE

*by* Andrew Gurr

*with* John Orrell

ROUTLEDGE
A Theatre Arts Book
NEW YORK

First published in 1989 in the United States of America by
Routledge/*Theatre Arts* Books
an imprint of Routledge Chapman and Hall Inc.
29 W. 35 Street, New York, NY 10001

**Library of Congress Cataloging-in-Publication Data**

Gurr, Andrew.
   Rebuilding Shakespeare's Globe.

   1. Globe Theatre (Southwark, London, England)
2. Theaters—England—London—History—17th century.
3. Theaters—England—London—Construction.
4. Shakespeare, William, 1564–1616—Stage history.
5. London (England)—Buildings, structures, etc.
6. Southwark (London, England)—Buildings, structures,
etc. I. Orrell, John. II. Title.
PR2920.G87    1989       792'.09421'64      89-5878
ISBN 0-87830-156-9

Designed by Peter Campbell

Printed in Great Britain

# CONTENTS

# ILLUSTRATIONS

*Frontispiece: The frontispiece from The Wits by Francis Kirkman, 1662. (British Library)*

*Title page: A detail showing the Globe from Wenceslas Hollar's drawing for his panorama of London published in 1647. (Yale Center for British Art, Paul Mellon Collection)*

[6]

[7]

its cloth of estate and canopy was the standard equipment for the royal 'presence'. (British Library)

# FOREWORD

The thoughts and the plans that are outlined in this book have been brewing for a long time. It is nearly two hundred years since the idea of reconstructing Shakespeare's own original playhouse was first proposed. Rebuilding it in London has been the dream of many people over the years. It became my dream when I first arrived in Southwark and found that the only record of Shakespeare's twenty-five amazing years of work in London was a bronze wall tablet. He needs, and we need, something more substantial than that.

This book is not the story of my efforts to get something more than a bronze tablet set up in Southwark to commemorate Shakespeare's work there. That story would occupy a book more than twice the length of this. It would describe endless successions of planning meetings, a world-wide fundraising campaign, a titanic struggle (an epic journey through an ocean of icebergs, though we managed not to sink). Above all, it would give due credit to the thousands of fine people who have given their support so unstintingly in the past twenty years as they helped the International Shakespeare Globe Centre to bring the dream into reality.

The title of the organization which was set up to make all this possible may seem a bit cumbersome. But it summarizes what we are and what we want: Shakespeare's Globe Theatre set in an international centre. The word 'international' reflects the extraordinary range of support we have had from London itself and throughout the world – not only the English-speaking world, from the USA to New Zealand, but everywhere that Shakespeare is admired, from Tokyo and Rome to Moscow and Warsaw. Shakespeare (I can't quite avoid the pun) is truly a global phenomenon.

This book is the story of what we are building. Its primary aim is to set out the case for what we are trying to do, and why we are doing it. The story of the steadily growing curiosity about Shakespeare's Globe over the centuries, the scholarly principles of authentic reconstruction, the state of our present knowledge about the business of play-acting which was Shakespeare's life's work in London: these, the basis and the justification for all our labours, are the first subject of this book. It goes on to analyse the crucial surviving evidence about the original design of the two playhouses which are being rebuilt as the central features of the complex: Shakespeare's own open-air amphitheatre, the Globe, and the hall theatre which Inigo Jones designed as an imitation of Shakespeare's second theatre, the Blackfriars. A final chapter describes our plans for the permanent exhibition, with its theatre models and its stage costumes, its audio-visual displays of Shakespearean performances telling the whole story of the original Globe playhouse which is the centrepiece of the whole complex, together with the actors, the playwrights, the patrons and the audiences which have brought the Elizabethan and Jacobean theatres gloriously to life through the ages.

This is not the place, in the book of the ISGC's plans, to single out the great contributions which so many enthusiastic helpers have so freely given to make it all possible. People from all over the world have given, with wonderful generosity, of both money and time. I hope to tell the story of this extraordinary display of truly intercontinental cooperation in a later book, when the complex is actually finished and in service. This is the book about the idea, the dream, and about the scholarly labours which turned the vague desire for a replica of Shakespeare's workshop into a reality. The work of the scholarly watchdogs Richard Hosley and John Orrell, on whose labours the rebuilt Globe's design largely depends, of Glynne Wickham and Andrew Gurr, the chief sponsors of the splendid international academic support we have enjoyed, underlies everything in this book. Above all, Theo Crosby, architect to the project, and chief negotiator between the demands of the scholars and the demands of practicality, deserves praise. We owe them all our special thanks for supporting the 'hard evidence' which is the essential foundation for the whole extraordinary project.

SAM WANAMAKER

# REBUILDING
# SHAKESPEARE'S
# GLOBE

## To the Reader.

This Figure, that thou here feeſt put,
   It vvas for gentle Shakeſpeare cut;
Wherein the Grauer had a ſtrife
   with Nature, to out-doo the life :
O, could he but haue drawne his vvit
   As well in braſſe, as he hath hit
His face ; the Print vvould then ſurpaſſe
   All, that vvas euer vvrit in braſſe.
But, ſince he cannot, Reader, looke
   Not on his Picture, but his Booke.

                                        B. I.

*1: Shakespeare, the Droeschoudt engraving made for the publication of Shakespeare's
plays in 1623, edited by his fellow-players John Heminges and Henry Condell.*

# CHAPTER ONE

# WHYS AND WHEREFORES

## 1. THE WHYS

When the Chamberlain's Company was formed in 1594, as one of the two companies licensed to perform plays for the general public in London, it had some powerful assets. Its patron, the Lord Chamberlain, was the member of the Privy Council responsible for the government's control of play-acting. Its leading player, Richard Burbage, was the young star of London's actors. His father was one of the two leading financiers of London's acting companies, builder of the first commercial play-houses and a former player himself. And its resident actor-playwright, a shareholder in the company, was William Shakespeare.

Despite all these great assets, though, the company went through difficult times in its early years. Not until a group of the company's leading players banded together in 1599 to help finance the building of the Globe was their prosperity assured. The Globe playhouse was both a major support for and a direct consequence of the talents of Shakespeare's company. The story of the Globe and the success of the plays Shakespeare designed for it go together.

The 1590s was a strange period for Londoners. In the country at large things were painfully hard. The last seven years of the century saw a succession of poor harvests, while the continuing war with Spain in the Netherlands drained the economy. In London itself throughout 1592 and 1593 the plague hit savagely, and the number of poor and needy grew fast, quite beyond the capacity of the London authorities to control them. At Court the Queen was ageing, and still refused to acknowledge any heir. The parliamentarian Peter Wentworth was imprisoned in the Tower in 1594 when he published a pamphlet arguing that James VI of Scotland should be named as Elizabeth's successor. Later in the decade the Earl of Essex began to make trouble, coming to see himself as Elizabeth's heir, a presumption that led him to attempt to raise London's citizens into rebellion in February 1601. But London also had a new phenomenon to wonder at and to feed its sense that the times were changing. For the first time there was a forum for airing important questions in public. Playhouses drew people in their thousands, and plays opened up a wealth of subjects for gossip and debate. Censorship made it necessary to be discreet, but since plays claimed to be fiction they mostly seemed incapable of giving direct offence.

In the 1590s it was not just a matter of finding a forum for the airing of new thoughts. For the past twenty and more years professional actors had been offering their brand of entertainment alongside the bear-baiting and bull-baiting in the suburbs. But then suddenly they had a Marlowe and a Shakespeare writing for them.

In the 1590s the experience of playgoing became not just a novelty for idle afternoons but a central feature of London life. The plays served as the newspapers of the day, staging versions of the latest battle across the Channel or the latest sensational murder. They could draw crowds of a size and a disposition never before seen in any city in Europe, and they could promote public debates about questions which had never before had a forum. The Earl of Essex himself knew the power inherent in the new excitement of playgoing. His supporters paid Shakespeare's company to perform *Richard II* the day before the rebellion, in order to remind Londoners of the story of a king deposed by his subjects for his wrongdoing. Essex saw himself as the figure of Bullingbrook, and thought that with the aid of Shakespeare's play he could become a king in the way that Bullingbrook became King Henry IV.

In a less directly political way, plays like *Romeo and Juliet* also offered a completely novel experience, one disturbingly capable of challenging traditional authority. *Romeo and Juliet* was one of the hits of the decade, at least in part because it argued in favour of marrying for love against marriage by parental choice. The habit of playgoing came to dominate London life in this decade. It made the government nervous, and provoked some severe restraints, but potentially it was hugely profitable and wonderfully promising for the players' purses. At first, however, Shakespeare and his fellow-actors had far from an easy ride.

By the time they built the Globe Shakespeare's company had worked together in four or five different playhouses, and had already suffered the loss of one new playhouse built especially for them. Beginning in May 1594 in an old playhouse in Newington Butts, a mile or more southeast of Southwark and London Bridge, they played for a short season at the Cross Keys Inn in Gracechurch Street inside the City before settling at the Theatre in Shoreditch, a playhouse built twenty years before by Richard Burbage's father. There they played successfully for two years, a success starred above all by the first appearance on stage of that most remarkable and popular of all Shakespeare's comic inventions, Falstaff.

*2: Falstaff, from* The Wits *by Francis Kirkman, 1662.*

Falstaff and his author must have been a strong reassurance to the company in its early years, because major problems soon confronted them. By the end of 1597 they had lost the Theatre, which was closed in a dispute over the renewal of its lease.[1] The underfunded company then moved to its lesser neighbour, the Curtain, and possibly also played at the new Swan playhouse on Bankside, where several of the members lived. Old Burbage had tried to replace his Theatre with a new playhouse in the City, built in a hall with a roof, unlike all the other amphitheatres. The project misfired badly and locked up his capital. By the time the company helped young Burbage to pull down the old Theatre and rebuild it on Bankside as the Globe, they had used five different playhouses in five years.

The company was a strange kind of organization, a mixture of trade guild and commune. Like the other playing companies it worked as a team, but with no real captain and certainly no manager. The 'sharers', the eight leading players, divided the various duties between them. They took collective decisions over company policy, whether it was a question of which play to perform or which playhouse to perform in. Most companies, once they established themselves in London, had a financier behind them, an impresario who usually owned the playhouse in which they performed, and often the stock of costumes and playbooks they performed with. Philip Henslowe was the leading impresario of the 1590s, having begun financing players as an extension of his bear-baiting activities in Southwark. The other major financier was James Burbage, who started as a player himself but by 1594 was supporting his son and the company to which he and Shakespeare belonged. It was the ruins of James Burbage's theatre-building enterprises which eventually created the Globe.

The Globe was the product of the company's collective talent – not just their acting ability but their willingness to work together by pooling their money as well as their skills. When old James Burbage lost his funds in his abortive attempt to build a hall playhouse in 1596, the company had to fall back on its own resources. The Globe was the first playhouse to be built by a playing company with funds largely supplied by its own members. Of the eight 'sharers' or co-owners of the company, six put up the cash for the Globe. Richard Burbage was one. He and his brother (not an actor), heirs of their father and therefore owners of the old Theatre's timbers, put up half the total cost. Shakespeare and four others put up the rest.[2]

*3: Richard Burbage, a portrait in the Dulwich Collection.*

The story of that financial adventure and the playhouse it produced is material for a later section of this book. But it reminds us of the unique significance of that first Globe playhouse. Not only did Shakespeare make a direct contribution to ensure that it could be built; he and his fellow-players took a direct share in its planning. The scheme evolved both from the painful shifts of the first five years of the company's existence and from Shakespeare's own experience writing his early plays for so many different playhouses. Its triumph, and the triumphant plays Shakespeare wrote for it, were created through the teamwork the company developed in the 1590s. Shakespeare's greatest plays– *Julius Caesar, Hamlet, Twelfth Night, Othello, Measure for Measure, King Lear, Macbeth, Antony and Cleopatra, Pericles, Cymbeline* and *The Winter's Tale*–were all written for the new playhouse which Shakespeare co-owned and helped to build in 1599.

No playwright has ever had more intimate knowledge of the playhouse for which he wrote his greatest plays. He helped to finance it and every working day he acted on its stage. As a 'sharer' in the company he performed in early Globe productions such as Jonson's 'Humours' plays, and performed kingly roles–including, so legend declares, the ghost in *Hamlet* – in his own plays. Shakespeare wrote, therefore, for a highly specific stage, a purpose-built machine, not for any theatre in the abstract nor for the printed page. Half of his plays never reached print until seven years after his death, and he never encouraged any of them into print in his lifetime, since printing the texts meant that other acting companies could make use of them. The Globe's stage was the sole means of publication he expected.

We lose or distort much of what is valuable in his plays so long as we remain ignorant of the precise shape of that playhouse, and of how Shakespeare expected his plays to be performed there. That is the chief reason for trying to reconstruct Shakespeare's Globe. Paper designs and models are some help, but not enough. A play in performance is a dynamic event, the product of a huge complex of details, from the penetrating quality of an actor's voice to the hardness of the bench a spectator may be sitting on or the state of the weather. We need to know these details, the precise shape of the stage

# This Comoedie was firſt
## Acted, in the yeere
## 1598.

### By the then L. CHAMBERLAYNE
### his Seruants.

## The principall Comœdians were,

| | |
|---|---|
| WILL SHAKESPEARE. | RIC. BVRBADGE. |
| AVG. PHILIPS. | IOH. HEMINGS. |
| HEN. CONDEL. | THO. POPE. |
| WILL. SLYE. | CHR. BEESTON. |
| WILL. KEMPE. | IOH. DVKE. |

4: The title page from Every Man in his Humour, 1598 (Folio 1616),
with the names of the original players.

and the auditorium, the quality of the light, the effects on sound and vision of an open-air arena and a crowded auditorium, the interplay between actors performing on a platform in an open yard and the packed mass of thousands of spectators, many of them standing, all in broad daylight. None of these effects, each of which influences the others, can be gauged without a full-scale reconstruction. Shakespeare's works were composed in full knowledge of the intricate and dynamic interplay through which his plays were to be performed at the original Globe. We owe it to ourselves to attempt some reconstruction of the more tangible features of that interplay.

In the later chapters of this book we will examine the evidence for

[19]

*Plate I: The Globe as it might have been in 1599. A bird's-eye view looking east towards*

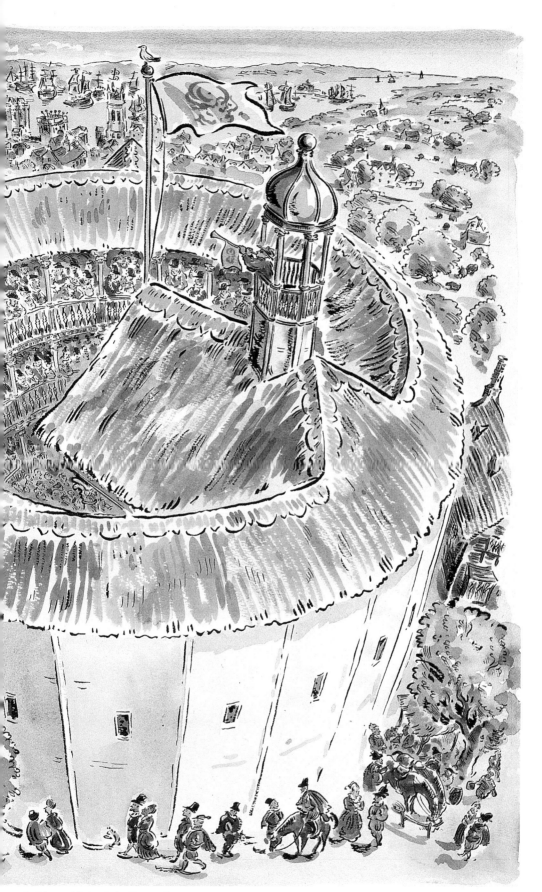

*London Bridge and the Tower. See note on p. 179.*

the shape of the original Globe and the calculations which have gone into the reconstruction planned for the Bankside. The design we have worked out for the rebuilt Globe is the product of many years of research, debate and calculation by hundreds of scholars. So far as we can tell, the Bankside reconstruction makes the best use of all the available evidence. It utilizes decades of scrupulous and sceptical combing of documents and illustrations. It applies all the information we have about Tudor techniques of building design and timberwork, the history of playhouse design as it evolved through the sixteenth century, as well as the hints in the plays themselves about the conditions they were written for. But it is not only a matter of designing a building. A thorough reconstruction, if it is to be properly useful, needs a specific location and well-informed users. These factors are the keys to the decision to rebuild the Globe in Southwark.

The geographical location of a rebuilt Globe is important in ways which became disconcertingly clear to its designers only when the design itself was under detailed consideration. That the Globe amphitheatre was open to the sky had been known for centuries, but the precise effect of sunlight on the performances only became an important question recently. The natural assumption for anyone to make, and especially for playgoers used to artificial light shining on the actors, was that London's reluctant and all-too-often invisible sun would have shone benignly down on the stage of the original Globe to light up its players through the daily performances between two and five in the afternoon. Only in 1979 was it realized that in fact the Elizabethan designers were careful to make sure the opposite happened.[3] The original builders fixed the stage at a point inside the circle of the galleries so that it had its back, not its face, to the afternoon sun. The 'shadow' or 'heavens' over the stage which kept the rain off the players also protected them from direct sunlight. The Globe's stage was aligned precisely with its back to the midsummer solstice, so that only a diffuse and shadowed daylight could fill the stage. The gallery roof was high enough to keep the sun out of everyone's eyes, players and audience alike, except for the few unfortunates sitting in the topmost gallery opposite the stage in midwinter, when the low

**Midsummer**
(+23½°)

**April/August**
(+11°)

**March/September**
(0°)

Orientation of Globe 48°

GMT

1pm

7pm

3pm

4pm

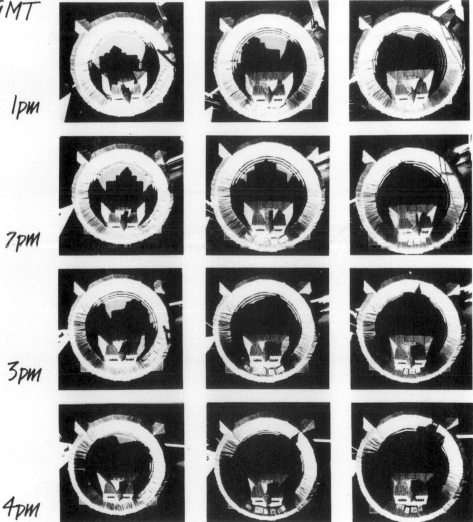

5: *Sunlight at the Globe, photographs of a model taken under the supervision of John Orrell and Theo Crosby at Pentagram Design, 1983.*

sun might reach them from behind the stage superstructure as the performance drew towards its close. Elizabethans did not like the sun. It gave pale London complexions a country look, and it faded the bright colours on expensive clothes. The players evidently disliked sunlight as well for its effect on their complexions and their costumes. Probably too—one of the questions the reconstructed Globe will test—the plays needed indirect daylight as a uniform background in the absence of any mechanism for lighting effects, except at the few points where night scenes were signalled by bringing on burning torches or candles.

It is this concern for sunlight at the Globe, added to the historical associations Southwark has enjoyed ever since Shakespeare began working there in 1599, which makes it so necessary to rebuild the Globe as close as possible to its original locality. The position of the sun through the year as it shone on the first Globe is unique to Southwark's latitude and longitude. So is the precise quality of the light, even indirect sunlight, as Shakespeare and his fellow players knew it and performed in it. An open-air amphitheatre at any other latitude would provide a different kind of light. The sun's exact movements through the sky, its position between 2 o'clock and 5 o'clock during performances, the characteristic local effects of cloud and the potent presence of the London weather pattern, are all aspects of the reconstruction unique to Southwark, and vital to its accuracy.

The physical location of the rebuilt Globe as close as possible to the original site is necessary to provide the original light and sound, vital elements in a daylight performance at an outdoor venue. But there are other elements nearly as vital and even less tangible which have to be considered. All the accuracy of a reconstruction of the physical environment for Shakespeare's plays is of little use without a reasonably accurate reconstruction of the conditions of performance, the complex interplay between what happens on the stage and the response in the auditorium. If this radical experiment of reconstructing Shakespearean performances of Shakespeare's plays is to work it needs actors who can abandon what they have been taught. They must learn from scratch the distinctive demands the Globe's peculiar construction lays on them. And, as much as actors, it needs audiences who can respond equally freshly to this strange way of experiencing the plays. The project is above all an educational experiment, an experiment in staging Shakespeare under conditions different from any London has known since the early seventeenth century. It is for people who can open themselves to the novel experiences this will bring. That is the main reason why the Globe itself is being built as the core of a large exhibition complex, an exhibition displaying the life and times of sixteenth-century playgoers. The total design is an educational milieu where the tangible environment can be recreated and experiments conducted to enable us to recover more of what Shakespeare, the genius of his age, did with and for his age.

The educational and experimental roles of the project are dependent on the Globe itself, and involve both of the chief components in a Shakespearean performance: actors and audience. The rebuilt playhouse will be a laboratory for actors to rediscover the art of acting in front of large crowds crammed into a small space, many of them watching and listening while on their feet, unable to ignore the people around them. Hamlet's soliloquies, these days usually spoken into the darkness by a solitary figure lit by a single spotlight, emphatically alone, must sound different when spoken in broad daylight on a high platform surrounded by hundreds of entirely visible listeners, some of whose ears are only inches from Hamlet's feet. The art of speaking soliloquies must have been very different for the Shakespearean player, compared with what modern actors understand. Modern audiences, too, accustomed to relaxing in soft armchairs in the dark where no twitch or grimace of reaction to what happens on stage can be seen, will need to learn new attitudes. The old music-hall tradition of comedians talking directly to the audience, and possibly even of audiences answering back and exchanging backchat with the performer, would put modern playgoers much more into the old frame of mind if it was revived at the rebuilt Globe. For all that Hamlet objected to the clown speaking more than was set down for him, Elizabethan clowns were expected to engage in what a contemporary called 'interloquutions with the audiences'.[4] Modern playgoers can only adjust to daylight performances and the vigorous high-speed delivery of Elizabethan players by divorcing themselves from the traditional expectations we take with us to our 'sacred' Shakespeare, where the audience sits in reverent silence and darkness, passive and withdrawn from the real activity of the interplay between the stage action and the responses required from the auditorium.

Modern re-creations of the Shakespearean kind of performance cannot be expected to replace or even seriously to alter the kind of performance offered by the Royal Shakespeare Company or the National Theatre, the new Globe's near neighbours. That tradition is too strong, too skilled and too distinctive to be directly affected by whatever these experiments in rediscovering Shakespeare may turn up. The effect on modern stagings of Shakespeare will be even more indirect. Modern audiences, like modern actors, are limited by a lifetime of training in a different kind of experience. Elizabethans were far more accustomed than we can ever be to learning by the ear rather than the eye, for instance. Stage 'spectacles' were a novelty – the Elizabethans invented the words spectacle and spectator, meaning viewers, to replace the older words audience and auditor, meaning hearers. But in their times the eye only slowly took over from the ear. Many of the members of the audience at the original Globe, especially the many women, were illiterate, and went to plays because hearing the words was the only form of learning, apart from sermons, that was open to them. So the central feature of the plays was speech.

The stage had no realistic scenery, only a set of curtains or 'hangings' against the rear wall, plus a few carry-on properties. Most of the setting as well as the story was conveyed through words. Moreover the words were delivered much faster than we are now used to hearing Shakespeare. Even on modern recordings, which need no more time for scene changing or intervals than Shakespeare provided, no play takes less than three hours. An uncut version of *Hamlet* such as Peter Hall's production for the opening of the National Theatre on the South Bank, would take more than four. In Shakespeare's time plays normally took little more than two hours. Jonson's *Bartholomew Fair*, along with *Hamlet* one of the age's most wordy plays, was claimed by Jonson himself to take only 'two houres and a halfe, and somewhat more'. [5]

[26]

The modern audience cannot be expected to hear Shakespeare, his language altered almost out of recognition by four hundred years of word-shifts, with the same ease an Elizabethan audience enjoyed. That fact, along with the introduction of fixed scenery after 1660 and the growth in the eighteenth century of the custom of providing intervals for refreshments, explains why we take Shakespeare so much more slowly now. But Shakespeare and Shakespeare's language are now the most widely shared element in school courses in every country where English is used. Shakespeare, it can be argued, is as familiar in the world today as he was in London in 1600. Audiences who go to the rebuilt Globe on Bankside in the 1990s will go because they know Shakespeare, and want to know more. Knowing more, by re-creating as much as we can of the conditions of the original staging, is the essential objective of the Globe project.

## 2. THE GROWTH OF THE IDEA

The idea of reconstructing Shakespeare's own playhouse is not new. It began in the nineteenth century as scholars learned more about the original staging and as the reader's interest in Shakespeare on the page began to mingle with the theatregoer's interest in Shakespeare on the stage. Plans to rebuild the Globe on Bankside emerged with strong support in the 1890s. In 1900 William Poel proposed to petition the London County Council for a site on which a replica of the Globe might be constructed. After the Boer War ended in April 1902 a specific proposal was put to them. This imaginative scheme, developed out of Poel's experiments with staging Shakespeare in the 1890s, was first shipwrecked by building regulations and then became hopelessly entangled in the arguments over a national theatre, which some advocates wanted to be based on Shakespeare's original play-house.[5] There was still a lot of doubt about the shape of the building, and even more uncertainty about the precise location of the site (not properly determined until W. W. Braines fixed it in 1924), but enthusiasm was mounting.

The desire to build a replica of the Globe partly grew out of dissatisfaction over the limitations of the traditional nineteenth-century theatre, with its fixed sets and proscenium arch. Traditional theatres and opera houses set plays in a 'picture frame' more suited to the eye than the ear, and took so long over scene-changing that much of the text had to be cut. In 1897, on the same day that Poel mounted a production of *The Tempest* which delivered the words without any scenery at all, George Bernard Shaw wrote a caustic protest about the current triumph of the eye over the imagination.

A superstitious person left to himself will see a ghost in every ray of moonlight on the wall and every old coat hanging on a nail; but make up a really careful, elaborate, plausible, picturesque, bloodcurdling ghost for him, and his cunning grin will proclaim that he sees through it at a glance. The reason is, not that a man can *always* imagine things more vividly than art can present them to him, but that it takes an altogether extraordinary degree of art to compete with the pictures which the imagination makes when it is stimulated by such potent forces as the maternal instinct, superstitious awe, or the poetry of Shakespeare.

Shakespeare's words, according to Shaw, stimulate the imagination while pictorial presentation only dampens it.[8] A visual show of a ship sinking on stage does not really heighten the excitement of the shipwreck scene which opens *The Tempest*.

*6: Beerbohm Tree's set for the opening scene of* The Tempest, *1903.*

[28]

*7: The hall screen in the Middle Temple dining hall.*

In 1894 Poel had founded the Elizabethan Stage Society, dedicated to performing Shakespeare in the original conditions. The Society's members sponsored readings of the plays, using only words and music, with no scenery. They also helped Poel to produce Shakespeare at the Inns of Court in London where Shakespeare's original company had performed them. Poel produced *Twelfth Night* for instance, in the hall of the Middle Temple, in front of the hall screen built in 1574. A young law student of the Middle Temple,

John Manningham, had recorded seeing the play at the Middle Temple in 1602 (he particularly enjoyed the gulling of Malvolio),[9] and Poel's production tried to reconstruct what the performance would have been like at that time. Similarly he reproduced a performance of *The Comedy of Errors*, which had been staged at Gray's Inn in 1594. The Elizabethan Stage Society created a kind of alternative Shakespeare, radically different from the standard London offerings of Henry Irving and Beerbohm Tree in the commercial theatre, which relied on spectacular scenery and cut the text drastically in order to make time for the spectacle. Poel rejected the static, visual Shakespeare that resulted, and argued for minimal staging with few properties and everything hanging on the words, as he felt the plays had had when they were originally performed at the Globe.

In the long run Poel's 'pure' Shakespeare had a profound effect on twentieth-century staging. He was admired by such influential stage designers as Edward Gordon Craig, who wrote an article advocating open-air theatres in 1911.[10] Perhaps most durably, he inspired Nugent Monck to build the Maddermarket Theatre in Norwich. Monck never ran professional theatre there, but he built a distinctive playhouse, a small-scale replica of what he thought an Elizabethan playhouse would have been like, with an apron stage. He also made it one of the seven theatres in the world ever to perform all of Shakespeare's plays.

All this served as a tremendous stimulus to young imaginations.[11] Between them, the chief supporters of this movement – Poel, Monck, Craig and Harley Granville Barker – led. the way from the Victorian actor-manager tradition of Irving and Tree to the 'director's theatre' which replaced it. Along with that development, which shifted the focus of attention from the actor to the director and his 'interpretation' of the play, went a shift from scenic Shakespeare to spoken Shakespeare. And with the shift, of course, there also went an upsurge of curiosity about the original staging and the original Globe.

In 1893 Poel remodelled the Royalty Theatre in London for his production of *Measure for Measure*, making it a 'fit-up' version of the playhouse which was first built as a rival to the Globe in 1600, Philip Henslowe's Fortune amphitheatre, for which the builder's contract

*8: The Maddermarket Theatre, Norwich.*

## PLAN AT AMPHITHEATRE LEVEL

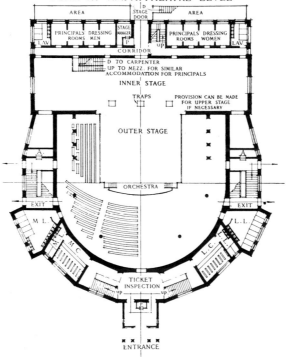

*9: The Mermaid Globe, drawings by Kenneth Cross, rendered by Cyril Faery.*

survives. More adventurously, in fact more fancifully, a half-sized replica of what the Globe was then thought to be like was designed in 1912 by that most fanciful of architects, Sir Edwin Lutyens. His design was built for the exhibition 'Shakespeare's England' at Earl's Court that year, at the prompting of the Shakespeare Memorial National Theatre Committee. This was the group originally formed as a result of a plea that Poel made during the Boer War. The Committee was still trying to knit the separate proposal for a National Theatre more closely around Shakespeare.[12] A company was formed to stage plays in Lutyens's replica, mostly doing short scenes, with a 'period' atmosphere created by boisterous apprentices in the audience, girls selling oranges and men selling stools to sit on. Poel produced a play there, and the manager, Patrick Kirwan, who had a company with a repertoire of Shakespeare plays (he later moved on to the Stratford Festival), mounted several there too.

Three times in the twentieth century war prevented plans to reconstruct the Globe in London from coming to fruition. The Boer War hampered Poel's initial scheme. The Shakespeare Memorial National Theatre project had moved no further than Earl's Court when the First World War broke out and stopped it. And then in the 1930s a much more substantial project came into being and got very near to success. The 1930s was a vigorous decade for theatre scholars, when rebuilding the Globe at last began to seem an entirely practical possibility. John Cranford Adams, basing his calculations on evidence now discredited but which at the time seemed thoroughly plausible, stirred imaginations both in London and the USA. The Chicago World Fair of 1933–34 displayed a large model of the Globe at the centre of its promenade area, where it stirred the imagination of the young Sam Wanamaker. Replicas were actually built at San Diego; in Odessa, Texas; for Iden Payne's Festival in Ashland, Oregon; in Cleveland, Ohio; in Cedar City, Utah; and at the Folger Shakespeare Library in Washington DC. The number of playhouses is a measure of the mounting enthusiasm. They had varying pretensions to accuracy as reconstructions of Shakespeare's original playhouse, of course. None of them had the peculiar geographical advantage of Southwark. That lay with the plans of the Globe-Mermaid Association of England

and America, which was formed in London in 1935.

In its way the Globe-Mermaid Association was a close precursor of the International Shakespeare Globe Centre. Its plan was to build a theatre, library and pub on the Bankside, on the site now occupied by Bankside Power Station. The complex was to comprise a replica of the Globe, a tavern to be called the Mermaid, designed with Tudor half-timbering, to recall the old legend of Jonson and the other poets drinking at the original Mermaid celebrated by Francis Beaumont in his famous poem, and a museum and library for Shakespeare studies. It was a prestigious scheme. Its president in England was the Marquess of Lothian, in the USA the President of Columbia University. Its vice-presidents included the US Ambassador to London Joseph P. Kennedy, Herbert Hoover, Viscount Leverhulme, Lord Tweedsmuir (John Buchan), Lord Bessborough and Jan Smuts. Among academics Dover Wilson, Allardyce Nicoll, Caroline Spurgeon, Tucker Brooke, W. L. Phelps and J. Quincy Adams were the chief official sponsors.[13] War, however, destroys many things. Among the smaller losses of the two World Wars fell London's two projects to reconstruct the Globe on Bankside.

There was much talk in 1951 before the Festival of Britain, that grand gesture of postwar resurrection set on the south bank of the Thames not far from the original Globe site. It was proposed to include a replica of the Globe among the new buildings. That scheme came to nothing, partly because recent scholarly work had cast doubt on the Cranford Adams models and the scholars needed time to find a new consensus about the original shape.[14] Close to another twenty years was needed for that. Not until 1970, under the energetic stimulus of Sam Wanamaker, who had been resident in Southwark since the 1950s, did the present scheme begin to seem feasible. In 1971 the first World Shakespeare Congress in Vancouver approved a proposal put by Glynne Wickham to support the project, and the work of gathering a scholarly consensus about the exact shape of a possible reconstruction began again.

# 3. SCHOLARLY STRUGGLES

In the nineteenth century the chief piece of evidence available which indicated what the shape of the Globe must have been like was a panorama of London engraved by C. J. Visscher. Visscher's 'View of London', published in 1616, shows a three-storeyed octagonal structure, as tall as it is broad, sloping inwards towards the top.

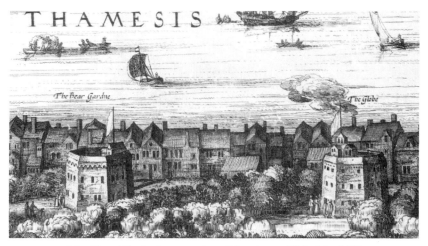

*10: Claes Visscher's engraving of London published in 1616, showing the Bear Garden and the Globe.*

Despite references from Shakespeare's own plays to the 'round Globe', to which could be added a depiction by John Norden dated 1593 showing round playhouses, and Wenceslas Hollar's etching of the second Globe, which shows a squat and perfectly circular amphitheatre, Visscher's tall eight-sided structure was assumed to be the best of the contemporary evidence.

Open-air amphitheatres were as much of an alien concept to nineteenth-century scholars as they were to playgoers. The impracticability of Visscher's tall, sloping structure therefore did not seem to be a problem. Then the discovery in 1888 of a drawing of the interior of an amphitheatre built close to the Globe on Bankside and only four years before it, Francis Langley's Swan playhouse, gave a strong boost to scholars because it presented a picture which people could make

*11: The second Globe, engraved by Wenceslas Hollar and published in 1644. In the original the captions for the Bear Garden and the Globe were accidentally reversed. In this reproduction the correct name has been restored.*

some sense of.[15] It was puzzling in many of its details—it still is—but for the first time a broadly recognizable shape, three levels of galleries surrounding a yard with a platform stage jutting out from one side, was available from the hand of an unquestionably authentic spectator of Shakespeare's own time. The Swan-drawing with its platform became the chief stimulus to Poel's reconstructions of the original staging.

Until 1923 many scholars, chiefly from Germany and the USA, made detailed contributions and added their assessments to the growing body of evidence. In that year a London civil servant working at the British Museum published a four-volume study, which he called, in plain terms, *The Elizabethan Stage*.[16] Sir Edmund Chambers was Second Secretary at the Department of Education, a post he served by absenting himself to work on his theatre history in the British Library for twenty years. Education's loss was Shakespeare's gain. In these volumes on Shakespeare's stage Cham-

tectum

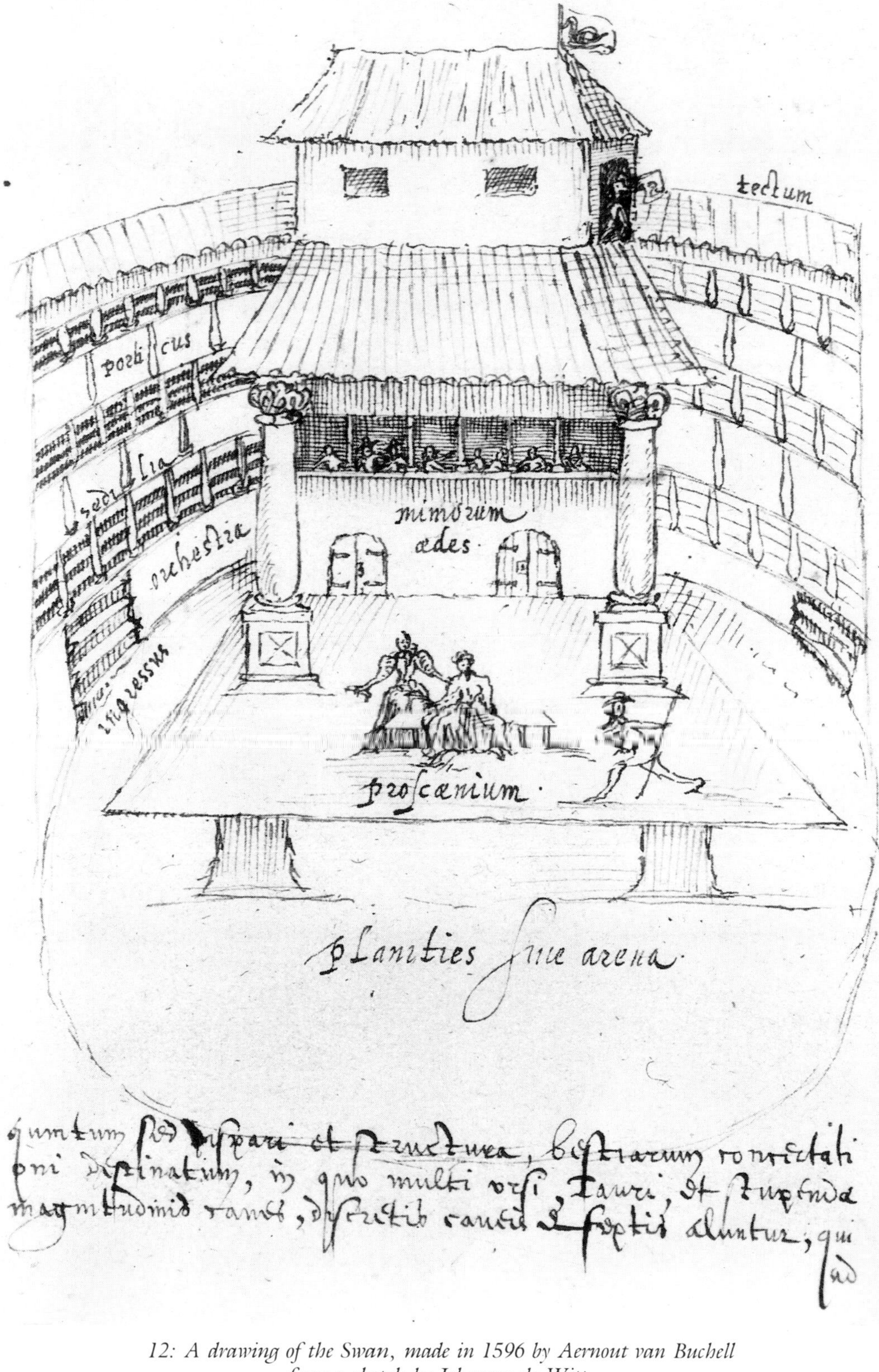

porticus

sedilia

orchestra

ingressus

mimorum
aedes

proscænium.

planties sive arena.

quintum sed disspari et structura, bestiarum concertati
oni destinatum, in quo multi ursi, tauri, et stupendæ
magnitudinis canes, distinctis caveis & septis aluntur, qui
ad

*12: A drawing of the Swan, made in 1596 by Aernout van Buchell
from a sketch by Johannes de Witt.*

bers gathered up all the existing evidence and summed up the many debates with crushing and succinct logic and authority. The weighty scholarship of his volumes as he drew together all the accumulated bits and pieces of evidence about the Globe and its neighbours gave an air of objective solidity to the subject. It swept away the imaginative if Swan-based concept of Lutyens, helping to make a serious and precisely accurate reconstruction appear feasible for the first time. It was to be, of course, nothing like so easy as that sounds.

Before 1923, in Germany and among the devotees of London's Elizabethan Stage Society, a rather odd new theory about Shakespearean staging had come into being. The original staging was recognized as being dependent on the words rather than on scenery, and the advantages of a continuous flow of scenes played on a platform in the middle of the audience was acknowledged. But scholars could not shake off modern expectations entirely. Even the least playgoing of Shakespeareans found it hard to ignore the long theatre tradition which separated the stage from the audience by a picture-frame or proscenium arch, and which used footlights and a curtain to mark that separation at the end of each scene and conceal the changes of scenery going on behind. The proscenium arch created an expectation that all indoor scenes must give the feeling of the indoors which the three-walled room of the picture-frame stage provided. Shakespeare's continuous staging acknowledged act and scene breaks only when the stage emptied momentarily and new characters entered. His plays had no intervals – indeed, there were no toilets for use at the intervals. In the nineteenth century it was impossible to conceive a play running non-stop in this way, with no pauses for the end of an act and no curtains for changes of scene. The picture-frame stage kept intruding on every attempt to conceptualize the Globe's original conditions for performance of the plays.

The first attempts to reconstruct Shakespeare's own staging settled for what has been called the 'alternation' theory. Seeing that most of the plays in the Renaissance tended to alternate crowd scenes where many characters were on stage with scenes of just one or two characters, scholars concluded that outdoor scenes for large groupings happened on the stage platform and alternated with indoor scenes and small numbers in a room or 'inner stage' at the back of the platform or on the balcony, on an 'upper stage'. They needed to think of indoor scenes taking place in a structure that was recognizably a room, as on a picture-frame stage. This led to the assumption that an indoor setting, a room of some kind, must have existed in the wall which the stage platform projected from, despite the absence of any such indoor area in the Swan drawing. Even after Chambers dismissed the theory of alternating scenes, the assumption about an indoor setting hung on. From the early 1920s until quite recently it was commonly assumed that the platform stage of the Swan drawing must have been backed by a room in which many complete scenes were acted, and that the Swan stage must therefore have been drawn inaccurately.

Using Visscher's octagon and the 'inner stage' assumption John Cranford Adams developed a brilliantly exact design, with precisely detailed dimensions, of a Shakespearean theatre. His work on a Globe plan, publicized through the 1930s when so many organizations were looking for an authoritative design, appeared in book form in 1942.[17] His meticulous and beautiful workmanship, aided by his friend and neighbour Irwin Smith, has been hugely influential.[18]

Unfortunately both of the principal guidelines Adams used as the basis for his model—Visscher's engraving and the theory of an inner stage—were soon to lose their credibility. Shortly before Adams's book appeared George Reynolds published a careful study of the plays written for the Red Bull amphitheatre which showed that an inner stage was not needed for any of the plays staged at that playhouse.[19] Then in 1948 I. A. Shapiro published a study of the early engravings of the Bankside playhouses.[20] He showed conclusively that most of them were based on Visscher and that Visscher's picture itself was quite unreliable. The long labour of calculating the Globe's real design had to begin again.

One picture of the Bankside which Shapiro did give credit to was Wenceslas Hollar's 'Long View' of both sides of the Thames. Hollar's etching had tended to confuse students of the Globe in two ways. First it showed the second Globe, the playhouse built as a replacement after the first Globe burned down in 1613. Some scholars felt

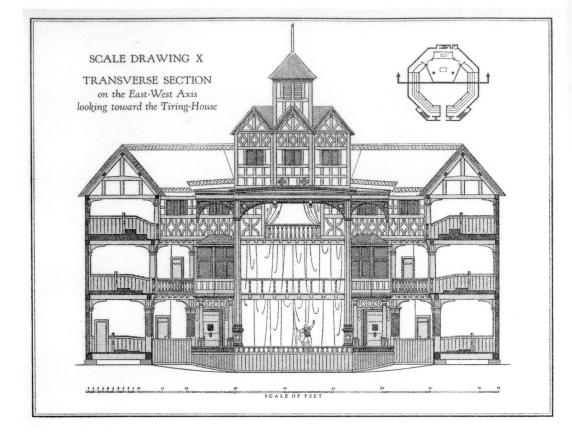

SCALE DRAWING X

TRANSVERSE SECTION
on the East-West Axis
looking toward the Tiring-House

SCALE OF FEET

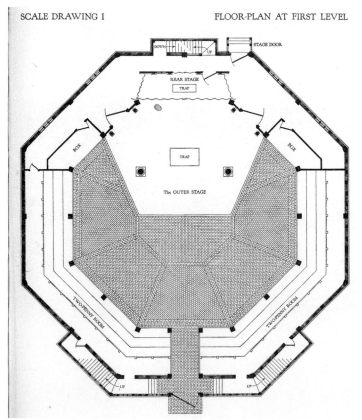

SCALE DRAWING I                    FLOOR-PLAN AT FIRST LEVEL

*13: Designs by Cranford Adams for his reconstruction of the Globe, published in 1942.*

that its round shape was too evidently a different building from the octagon which Visscher's picture claimed the first Globe was, despite the existence of documents which said that the second was built on the foundations of the first. And also, when the plates for the 'Long View' were engraved from Hollar's pencil drawings in Amsterdam, the captions for the two amphitheatres visible in Southwark, the Globe and the bear-baiting arena, had been accidentally reversed. It was an easy mistake to make, since etchings are made as a mirror image of the final picture, but it hardly encouraged confidence in Hollar, who was in any case out of London when the engraving was made. Even after W. W. Braines pointed the mistake out in his book about the site of the Globe, scholars remained reluctant to trust Hollar. Not until John Orrell published his examination of the 'Long View' in 1982 was Hollar's quite outstanding precision and the exactitude of his measurements made clear.[21] Hollar's etching of the second Globe, and more specifically his pencil drawing from which the etching was made, is now seen as a much better indication of the shape of the original Globe than Visscher's tall octagon.

14: *A detail from Hollar's 'Long View' of London, showing Southwark, including the Bear Garden and the Globe (captions reversed).*

[41]

The full story of the debate over the seventeenth-century pictures of the Globe is told in Chapter Three. Many scholars have contributed to the debate, and to the broad consensus about the design which began to emerge in the 1980s. Richard Hosley, Glynne Wickham and John Orrell, working in the USA and Canada as much as in Britain, are the principal architects of the consensus and the chief advisers for the present scheme. By 1986 five major seminars had been held at Pentagram, the office of the project architect Theo Crosby, to advise on details of the design. These seminars were attended by the leading scholars of Shakespearean playhouse design from all around the world, together with experts on Tudor building traditions, actors, directors and teachers of Shakespeare.[22] The designs described in Chapter Five of this book are the outcome of that consensus, cemented by the tenacity, sagacity and experience of Theo Crosby, the architect.

# 4. THE GLOBE REBUILT

Given the fragile and fragmentary nature of much of the evidence about the Globe's original design, the reconstruction described in this book must necessarily be regarded as conjectural. It is simply the best-informed conjecture that the present state of our knowledge allows us to provide. Always we maintain the hope that more information will appear. It may come from archaeology – digging up some fragments of the original foundations for instance – or from library research, turning up some long-lost paper in the way that the Dutch Johannes de Witt's drawing of the stage of the Swan playhouse, made on his visit to London in 1596, was found in 1888. Any reconstruction involves some elements of guesswork, and this scheme necessarily depends on quite a few guesses to fill gaps in our knowledge. It is an experiment. Without having tried to reconstruct the original shape we should know far less than we do at the present time about Shakespeare's Globe. The huge labour of turning the fragments of evidence into a full-scale, practical piece of architectural design has already revealed far more about the original design than any study of the fragments alone could have done. But it remains a conjecture, an experiment in designing what we think Shakespeare might have wanted for his plays in 1599. How effective an experiment it is will depend on what the whole project can tell us when it is in full operation. Building the Globe only provides the equipment. The final experiments can only begin once the Globe is available for staging plays in front of an audience willing to endure the Elizabethan audiences' discomforts.

The Globe reconstruction itself is first and foremost the centrepiece of a display of theatre history. Visitors to the complex will be able to follow three stories, each converging on the Globe playhouse from a different direction. They will see a comprehensive exhibition of sixteenth-century Southwark and the City of London, its houses and streets, its workplaces and its recreations. Secondly they will be able to trace the history of playhouse design, from models of the early playhouses to the details of the Globe itself, and the later hall playhouses which succeeded it. And thirdly they will be able to trace Shakespeare's own career from Stratford to his becoming a player and poet in London, his residence in Southwark and his apartment in the old gatehouse at Blackfriars. The life of the city, the life of the player and the evolution of the playhouse in which the city enjoyed his plays are the three stories of the exhibition. Their meeting point is the reconstruction of the Globe itself.

Centrepiece though it is, the playhouse on its own is just a shell. It was built for playing, and to see the building without a play being performed in it is to have only a part of the full experience. The standard time for an Elizabethan performance to begin was about 2 pm by the sun and by Greenwich Mean Time. Under British Summer Time (from March to October) in London, through the season when the weather is most likely to make outdoor playgoing a pleasure, this means 3 pm. A complete experience of the exhibition must conclude with a late afternoon performance at the Globe, where one must hope that British Summer Time lives up to its name. The plays staged there will mostly be Shakespeare's own, and they must be performed by actors who have themselves experimented with the alien conditions the Globe imposes on modern actors. They will offer continuous

V

*Plate II: The Globe as it might have been in 1599. A view of the stage from the yard. See note on p. 180.*

staging (no pause for act or scene breaks or interval), acting at high speed to an audience either sitting or standing in full view, and 'strong' acting to cope with the demands of open-air acoustics and an audience concentrating exclusively on the actors and their words, listening on their feet.

A new tradition of ensemble playing will have to develop to cope with the complex, novel and probably unforeseeable demands on acting in the Globe repertory. Much more will depend on the actors than on the staging or on any elaborately predetermined features of 'production'. It will certainly not be the now-standard 'director's theatre'.

The exhibition stories which will lead up to the Globe itself are by no means the whole story of Shakespeare's playhouse. In 1608 Shakespeare was writing *Cymbeline* and had not yet begun to think about *The Winter's Tale* and *The Tempest*. In that year his company finally secured the hall playhouse in Blackfriars which the Burbages had originally thought would make the Globe unnecessary. They had been blocked from using it for more than twelve years, and in the meantime it had been leased to a boy company, which catered to a much wealthier clientele than the Globe.[23] The cheapest seats at the Blackfriars cost sixpence, the price of a 'lords' room' at the Globe. Just to get in cost six times what it cost to put an 'understander' on his feet around the Globe platform. It catered to a smaller, much more 'select' audience, and it brought in more money. Had Shakespeare's company been able to use the Blackfriars playhouse in 1596 when it was first built for them, they would never have built the Globe. The full story of how the Blackfriars fiasco led to the building of the Globe is told in the next chapter. So far as the exhibition's story is concerned, the story of the Blackfriars alternative belongs alongside that of the Globe (indeed, on both sides, before and after) and is intricately bound up with Shakespeare's career as a professional playwright.

The boy companies made much less from the Blackfriars than Shakespeare's company was later to do, because whereas the adult companies performed daily the boys performed only once a week. In 1608, in trouble over plays which offended the king, as well as because of their limited income, the managers of the boy company surrendered their lease to the Burbages. From then on Shakespeare's company had two playhouses to perform in. Shakespeare's last plays were written for the two playhouses, and *The Tempest* apparently only for the Blackfriars.[24]

From 1609 until all the playhouses were closed in 1642, Shakespeare's company did what with hindsight seems the sensible thing. In summer, from May to September, they performed to the three thousand people who had been in the habit since 1599 of cramming themselves into the Bankside playhouse. For the seven months of shorter daylight hours and colder weather they performed indoors at the Blackfriars. Something—perhaps a real affection for the playhouse which had seen their first glorious years, probably a continuing loyalty to the penny-paying 'understanding men' of the Globe's yard, quite possibly also a degree of doubt about whether the more privileged audience at the Blackfriars would like them, or most likely a combination of all these thoughts made them undertake this unique and extravagant policy of dividing their year between two playhouses.

The Globe itself and its first ten dazzling years certainly did secure the affection of the players. The evidence for that appeared a few years later when the original cut-price idea of roofing the galleries with thatch proved to have been a false economy, and it caught fire, burning the playhouse to the ground. Faced with that loss they could easily have left the embers and turned to performing all the year round in their other playhouse. That would certainly have made better financial sense than the course they did adopt. Once again they dipped into their pockets. They rebuilt the Globe more lavishly than before. It was a massive, almost monumental testimony to the importance of the Globe in the minds of its players.

That being so, the story of the Globe is incomplete without an account of the second Globe and the Blackfriars, and the other hall playhouses which came to rival the amphitheatres after 1608. Regrettably there is even less hard evidence about the Blackfriars playhouse than there is about the Globe. The hall's main dimensions are known, together with the fact that it had two or three rows of curved

[47]

galleries.[25] It had boxes for the most important playgoers, particularly the ladies of the Court, alongside the stage. It allowed a few gallants to sit on the stage itself on stools hired for the purpose. It had chandeliers to supplement the light from the windows which shone on the auditorium and the stage. The rest of its physical appearance is largely a matter of conjecture. Logically it might be possible to attempt the same act of reconstruction for the Blackfriars as for the Globe. But the recent discovery of a peculiarly comprehensive piece of detailed evidence about a similar playhouse has created a unique new opportunity instead.

Various items of evidence have survived about all of the nine amphitheatres and five hall playhouses built for paying playgoers between 1567 and 1629.[26] For only one, though, has a complete set of plans survived. They were drawn up in about 1616 by Inigo Jones, the King's Surveyor. It was in that year that the first hall designed as a rival to the Blackfriars was built, the Cockpit in Drury Lane. Jones's plans were very likely drawn up for the Cockpit; even if what was built in Drury Lane was not precisely what he planned, the design stands as his concept of what would have made a practicable playhouse in 1616, fit to rival the Blackfriars.[27] So along with the reconstruction of the Globe will go the construction of Jones's plans for a hall playhouse. It may seem perverse to ally the reconstruction of the Globe not with the Blackfriars but with its chief rival. To miss the opportunity of building such a playhouse when we have a version of its original plans, though, would be a crime. Conjectural reconstructions are valuable experiments. The Jones plans are a reality.

The full story of the Inigo Jones plans and their identification in the 1970s is told in Chapter Four. In the project as a whole, the Jones playhouse provides a special link between the Shakespearean age and modern theatres in England. Built in the year Shakespeare died, it was not only one of the last two playhouses to open in that prolific era, but it was the only playhouse which offered a challenge to the supremacy of the Blackfriars in the last years up to 1642. It was also the only playhouse from the Shakespearean period to reopen in the Restoration. It became, in fact, in 1660, the first playhouse with a proscenium arch in London.[28] Jones's plans give us a unique

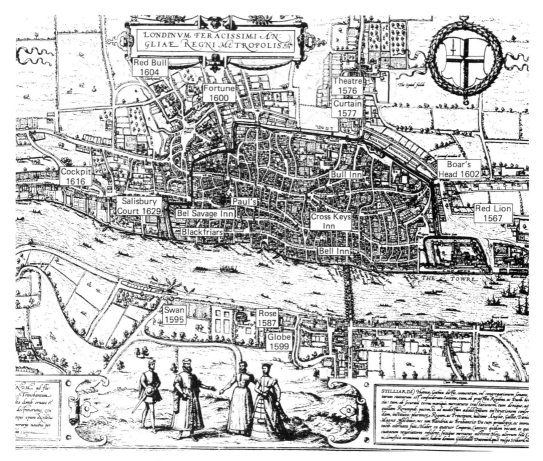

15: *An engraving of London published in 1572. The approximate positions of the major playhouses built between 1567 and 1629 are given, with the dates of construction.*

transitional form, the perfect setting for the story of what happened to Shakespearean staging after 1608 and in the Restoration period after 1660.

The main differences between amphitheatres like the Globe and hall playhouses like the Blackfriars and the Cockpit are matters for consideration in later chapters. In the exhibition the story of the amphitheatres and of the Globe itself will largely precede the view of the full-scale reconstruction of the Globe. The story of the Blackfriars and later developments will be focused on the Inigo Jones hall in an optional extension of the trail.

The third and by far the most extravagant kind of playhouse the Shakespearean players used was the theatres made available to them for performances before the royal Court. At Whitehall under the Stuart kings, the Christmas season of plays at Court was lavishly extended from Elizabeth's rather frugal fare. Shakespeare's company, its pre-eminence acknowledged by the title James granted them in 1603, the King's Men, performed as often at Court as all the other playing companies put together. Staged at night, unlike the Globe and Blackfriars performances, Court performances were expensive affairs. Different venues were employed (the company was highly mobile, as it had to be, running from the Bankside to perform for the Court at Whitehall or Greenwich on the same day), and detailed records have survived about some of the venues. One playhouse in particular, converted in 1629 from an old cockfighting pit which was sometimes used to stage Court plays, is well recorded in a copy of Inigo Jones's own design. The 'Cockpit at Court', where the King's men performed *A Midsummer Night's Dream*, *Volpone*, *Philaster* and many others of their plays through the 1630s, represents a high point in pre-Restoration stage design.[29] A model of this second Inigo Jones playhouse, together with dioramas of Court staging, is a feature of the exhibition's final display.

The whole exhibition, with its two life-size playhouses as integral parts of the story, is only one section of the resources to be assembled at the Bankside. To provide a record of living theatre and to offset the live performances on the Globe and Inigo Jones stages, the project is assembling a huge archive of Shakespeare in performance. Audio and

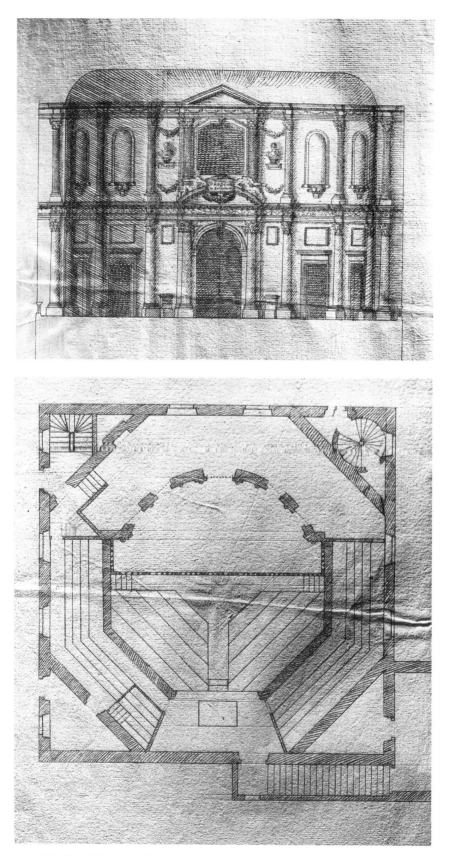

16: *The Inigo Jones designs for the Cockpit at Court in Whitehall, 1631.*

video records of past performances around the world, and cinema and television versions of the plays, are lodged with the project, and selections will be on show in the small cinema in the basement. This audio-visual archive will be constantly replenished, and will be linked with the major archives holding Shakespeare in performance in Britain and the USA. A reminder that Shakespeare's work was and still is a performing art, it will provide a means of comparing the Shakespeare of the original Globe with the multitude of rich variants in different media created in the twentieth century.

From its fraught and underfunded origins, through the first triumphant resurrection built by the players' faith in 1614, to its re-creation on twentieth-century Bankside, the Globe has stood as a symbol completely worthy of its name. The players may very well have felt a wry sense of the special aptness of the picture they put on their flag at its opening in the early summer of 1599: Hercules bearing the celestial globe on his shoulders. To build their own playhouse had been indeed a labour of Hercules, in some sense. Rebuilding it has been no less a labour, lasting more than twenty years and involving the efforts of far more than the three thousand people the original Globe could entertain inside its wooden O. It is to be hoped that this Herculean labour will provide rewards as great now as the players found it gave them then.

# CHAPTER TWO

# THE GLOBE IN 1600

## 1. AUDIENCES IN 1600

What sort of playgoers went to the first Globe, and what did they find? We know it could hold about three thousand spectators, a thousand of them on their feet standing around the flanks of the stage in the yard, the rest on benches in the surrounding galleries. We know performances were continuous, with no intervals, that food and drink were sold during the performance, and that the play began at 2 o'clock in the afternoon and concluded with a jig or song-and-dance act at about 5 pm. The conditions and the time of day were closer to those for a modern football match than a play.

Those are the most obvious differences. Much less obvious are the small details which belonged uniquely to the time of original performance and cannot so easily be reproduced today. At the first performances of *Hamlet*, for instance, on the two occasions when Hamlet contrasts his own inaction with the vigour of Hercules, the classical man of action, the audience would have recognized Hamlet's image of Hercules carrying the celestial globe on his shoulders as the emblem on the playhouse flag. Consequently they might register more quickly than we can Hamlet's sense of being out of place in a world which needed a Hercules to right its wrongs. The more regular playgoers who heard Polonius claiming that he had played Julius Caesar at the university, and Hamlet joking about the 'brute' part of the man who assassinated him, might have recognized in the actor now playing Polonius the same actor who had played Caesar at the Globe the year before, and the actor now playing Hamlet as Brutus in the other play. It might have led them to expect that this 'brute' actor

[53]

might repeat his former action, and kill Polonius as he had killed Caesar, which he does in the next scene.

The original audiences would also have seen Hamlet's soliloquies addressed directly to the visible 'understanders' around the stage. Watching the play in open daylight they would be more conscious of the playhouse surroundings, and more eager than we now need to be to use their imaginations to strengthen the illusion. The first twelve lines of *Hamlet*, spoken in broad daylight on a warm afternoon, told them that the air was bitterly cold and the time midnight. The early audiences had to believe the illusion, but the evidence to remind them that it was only illusion was far more visible and tangible all around them than it is in darkened modern theatres.

The original experience of playgoing was quite well documented in comments by writers of the time, and especially by visiting tourists. In September 1599 Thomas Platter, a young Swiss gentleman from an educated family who was visiting England to broaden his education, went to see a play at the recently opened Globe. He saw *Julius Caesar*, a new play of that year, and reported home about the experience.

On 21 September after lunch, about two o'clock, I and my party crossed the water, and there in the house with the thatched roof witnessed an excellent performance of the tragedy of the first Emperor Julius Caesar with a cast of about fifteen people. When the play was over they danced marvellously and gracefully together as their custom is, two dressed as men and two as women.

He also described the basic facilities for playgoers.

The playhouses are built so that they perform on a raised platform, in order that everyone has a good view. There are different galleries and places, though, where the seating is better and more comfortable, and therefore more costly. Whoever cares to stand below pays only one English penny, but if he wishes to sit he enters by another door and pays a second penny, while if he desires to sit on the most comfortable seats with a cushion he pays yet another English penny at another door. And during the performance food and drink are taken round the audience, so that one may also buy refreshments.

Besides the yard where the price of admission was one penny, and the 'twopenny galleries' as they were called, there were also special rooms on the balcony over the stage, known rather grandly as 'lords' rooms'. They cost sixpence, and could hold no more than three or four of the wealthier spectators each. Admission to these rooms was through the players' tiring house or dressing room behind the stage, and was usually confined to the genuinely noble customers or those young 'gallants' who wished to show themselves and their fine clothes to the rest of the audience. The lords' rooms made it difficult for other spectators not to see them, since they were positioned over the stage flanking the balcony room from which Juliet would call for Romeo. They completed the circle of audience. It was theatre in the round.

The Globe was a 'popular' playhouse. Its three thousand customers were distinct chiefly by their numbers. In deliberate contrast to this, the much smaller indoor playhouses like the Blackfriars and the Cockpit catered for quality rather than quantity. The difference in the price of a seat was enough to emphasize this. The open-air playhouse catered for the whole social range, and relied mainly on large numbers of customers for its income. It is at the Globe that we might expect to see the whole spectrum of London society on display.

In 1600 London was a fast-growing city, the largest and one of the

*17: The audience on the balcony of a hall playhouse, from the title page of* Roxana, *1632.*

most prosperous in Europe. Its population grew from 100,000 in 1580 to 400,000 in 1650. Its wealth was concentrated in the City, where the aristocracy and wealthy merchants and employers lived. In 1600 this wealth was spreading west into Westminster, and early in the seventeenth century it spread into Bloomsbury to cover what is now the West End. The poor classes, artisans and craftsmen and the many unemployed, including a mass of immigrants from the country-side who came to London in search of work, lived in the outlying suburbs. These began outside the City walls, and by 1650 stretched for several miles to the north, east and south. In 1600 the poorest suburbs were to the north and east. The south bank of the Thames was slower to grow as a residential area, and was most noted as a place for recreation, with its bear-baiting amphitheatre, its playhouses and its whorehouses.[2] Eastwards from the Archbishop of Canterbury's palace at Lambeth much of Southwark was owned by the Bishop of Winchester. The popular name for London whores was 'the Bishop of Winchester's geese'.

London's geography was important to the builders of playhouses, because the Lord Mayor and Corporation at Guildhall were consistently hostile to them. The players performed in the afternoons when men ought to be at work, and they attracted large crowds at a time when there was not yet any organized police force to control such numbers. The Lord Mayor never allowed any playhouses to be built inside the territory he controlled, and by 1595 he had even managed to secure the Privy Council's consent to a ban on players performing at the inns inside the City, which they had been doing whenever possible for the previous thirty years. Consequently the amphitheatres had to be built in the poorer suburbs to the east and north of the City, which were under the more easygoing jurisdiction of the Middlesex magistrates, and later on Bankside, controlled by the Surrey magistrates. The only playhouses to escape this embargo were the first hall playhouses, catering for much smaller numbers and attracting wealthier customers. St Paul's churchyard had a playhouse in intermittent use between 1575 and 1605, and two playhouses were built in halls in the 'liberty' of Blackfriars, inside the City walls but outside the Lord Mayor's jurisdiction. One of these ran from 1576 to

1590, and again from 1599 to 1605, the other from 1600 to the final closure in 1642. Three more outside City walls, one of them in Drury Lane and two in Whitefriars in the wealthy West End, were also in use between 1608 and 1642. The greatest of these halls, the second of the two Blackfriars playhouses, was originally built in 1596 for Shakespeare's company when the Lord Mayor stopped the use of City inns, though the company did not get access to it until 1609. In the interim, from 1600, it was used for weekly performances by a boy company.

From 1590 until two boy companies re-started playing, at Paul's in 1599 and the Blackfriars in 1600, only the amphitheatres were available for playgoing. Accounts of the time suggest that the whole spectrum of London's society contributed playgoers to the first gatherings at the Globe. In the audience which Platter joined for *Julius Caesar* in September 1599 there might have been apprentices and the unemployed from the lowest financial levels, house servants, unskilled labourers (porters and carters, seamen and soldiers, fishwives and applewives). With a little more affluence there were artisans (skilled handicraft workers), and further up the scale of wealth citizen employers, merchants, law students from the Inns of Court, military officers, gentry and lords. Women were a major presence, and included a range from whores through citizen wives to Court ladies.

John Davies wrote an epigram in 1593 using a playhouse crowd as a simile for a thorough mixture of people from the whole of London's society:

> For as we see at all the play house dores,
> When ended is the play, the daunce, and song
> A thousand townsemen, gentlemen, and whores,
> Porters and serving-men together throng ...[3].

Given the time of performance, in the middle of the working day, it is the presence of 'townsemen'–citizen employers, craftsmen and apprentices–which is the most surprising feature of this gathering. Idle men and women could be expected to attend the most popular form of public entertainment in town. Thomas Nashe wrote in 1592 that

whereas the after-noone being the idlest time of the day ... men that are their owne masters (as Gentlemen of the Court, the Innes of the Courte, and the number of Captaines and Souldiers about *London*) do wholy bestow themselves upon pleasure, and that pleasure they devide (howe vertuously it skils not) either into gameing, following of harlots, drinking, or seeing a Playe.[4]

But apprentices were not expected to be idle. Indentured for seven years, they worked without pay, only receiving board and lodging, to learn their trade, whether as leatherworkers, grocers, mercers, goldsmiths or any of the other guild occupations in London. Even the penny admission to an amphitheatre for the apprentices was hard-earned, and largely a matter of their employer's generosity. And yet apprentices, especially in the poorer handicraft trades, were as conspicuous a presence in the playhouse audiences as the law students and gentlemen from the Inns of Court on the west side of the City. The apprentices could not pay the sixpence admission to a hall playhouse as the gentlemen could, but at the amphitheatres they made up in numbers what they lacked in financial resources.

Until James Burbage built the Blackfriars in 1596 the main priority which he and the other impresarios worked on was the basic and minimal level of provision, what the apprentices' penny could buy. Most of the players, including Burbage himself, had started their careers travelling the country with their plays, performing in marketplaces or guildhalls, wherever they could draw a big enough crowd to justify putting up their stage platform. Audiences stood around the stage. Any gallery or seating accommodation there might be in the marketplace or innyard was an incidental extra. Except for the change introduced by the building of the first London amphitheatres, which allowed the players to collect the pennies at the door before the play started, that continued to be the model for the London players until 1609. The basic provision was standing room in the yard around the stage. The galleries were a bonus. If you wanted a seat, a cushion, a roof over your head, you paid twopence or more and removed yourself to the back of the crowd.

James Burbage's Blackfriars playhouse inverted these priorities. At his new playhouse everyone had a seat and the more you paid the closer you sat to the stage. For the basic sixpence you had a bench in the most distant gallery. To sit in the 'pit' near the stage, the equivalent of the amphitheatre yard, you paid three times the gallery price. For five times the gallery price you could have a box flanking the stage. Burbage's priorities at his amphitheatres, including the Globe, favoured the mass of the poorest spectators, whereas at the Blackfriars priority was given to the most wealthy and the poorest people were removed to the places furthest from the stage. This, a priority still reflected in modern theatres, did not become available to Shakespeare's company until the Globe had been in operation for ten years. That decade of success was the reason that the Globe was never supplanted by the Blackfriars as Burbage originally meant it to be, and that for thirty-three years the two ran in partnership. The Globe was rightly called the 'popular' playhouse of its time.

*18: A London merchant's wife, engraved by Hollar, from the early 1630s.*

# 2. PLAYGOING IN 1600

Throughout Shakespeare's lifetime plays were available for Londoners every day of the week except Sunday, and all the year round except in Lent. Playgoers could learn what plays were to be performed from handwritten playbills stuck up daily on posts around the City. The playgoing fare was 'Painted in play-bills, upon every post', as a play belonging to Shakespeare's company put it in 1599.[5] If it was a new play it might cost twice the normal price. Usually each playhouse offered a different play each day so that anyone with the leisure and the habit of 'attending plaies dailie' could do so without risk of repetition. The lists of performance through the 1590s at the rival playhouse to Shakespeare's indicate that no play was staged more than two or three times in any month, and only the most popular approached twenty performances in a year.

As the time of performance drew near, after the 11 am mealtime for citizens and the midday meal of the gentry,[6] the playhouses began to make signals to their prospective clients. Each playhouse ran up its flag, the Globe's easily visible across the river to anyone looking from the City for it. Access to the amphitheatres and for the Globe's poorer patrons was on foot, up Gracechurch Street to the old Shoreditch playhouses, through Cripplegate to Golden Lane and Finsbury for the Fortune, or down Gracechurch Street and across London Bridge to the Rose, the Swan and the Globe. Wealthier patrons heading for the Globe and its neighbours made use of the nearest thing London then had to a taxi service, paying sixpence to be rowed in one of the thousands of wherries across from Paul's Wharf or Whitehall Stairs to the riverbank in Southwark.

For the watermen ferrying playgoers was a major source of income. In 1614 when only the Globe was still offering plays on the Bankside, the poet John Taylor, a waterman himself, complained sadly about the loss of business for the ferrymen. The transfer of the Rose's business to the playhouses in the north meant that 'every day in the weeke they doe drawe unto them three or four thousand people, that were used to spend their monies by water.'[7] Taylor was inflating the

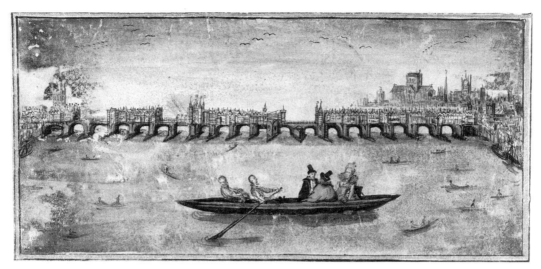

*19: A ferry on the Thames, with passengers.*

Sala Regalis cum Curia weſt monaſtery *vulgo* Weſtminſter haall

*20: Coaches in Whitehall, an engraving by Hollar.*

numbers to make his point, but he was right about the shrinkage of revenue among the watermen.

By 1614, though, there were other forms of transport to the playhouses, and other problems. The ferries were always the chief means of transport to the Globe – Sir Humphrey Mildmay's diary records him paying sixpence for a boat every time he went to see a play at the Globe in the 1630s[8] – but for the northern playhouses and especially the hall playhouses in Blackfriars and Drury Lane from about 1605 onwards the luxurious form of travel was by coach. And that meant traffic jams. A petition by the residents of Blackfriars in 1619 was eloquent on the subject:

there is daylie such resort of people, and such multitudes of Coaches (whereof many are Hackney Coaches, bringinge people of all sortes) that sometymes all our streetes cannott containe them. But that they Clogg up Ludgate also, in such sort, that both they endanger the one the other breake downe stalles, throwe downe mens goodes from their shopps. And the inhabitantes there cannott come to their howses, nor bringe in their necessary provisions of beere, wood, coale, or haye, nor the Tradesmen or shopkeepers utter their wares, nor the passenger goe to the common water staires without danger of their lives and lymmes.[9]

All attempts by Guildhall and the Privy Council to control the use of coaches by the wealthy had little effect. A newsletter of 1634 reported that the Blackfriars traffic jams were still intolerably troublesome, and that parking regulations had little effect.

Here hath been an Order of the Lords of the Council hung up in a Table near *Paul's* and the *Black-Fryars*, to command all that Resort to the Play-house there to send away their Coaches, and to disperse Abroad in *Paul's Church-Yard*, *Carter Lane*, the Conduit in *Fleet-Street*, and other Places, and not to return to fetch their Company, but they must trot afoot to find their Coaches, 'twas kept very strictly for two or three Weeks, but now I think it is disorder'd again.[10]

When the Blackfriars playhouse closed for the summer and the players transferred to the Globe, both the ferrymen and the Blackfriars locals had good reason to be grateful.

By whatever form of transport playgoers got to the Globe, as they came closer to the building they were hastened along by noise as well as by the sight of the flag. A trumpeter perched on the roof hurried latecomers along.

Once everyone was inside, the three-knocks which are still traditional in French theatres would silence the chatter and announce the entry of the Prologue or the players to start the performance. All questions of personal comfort, a seat with a cushion, a good view past the head of the person in front, would be settled before the play began. If it looked like rain a choice had to be made between either saving money and getting wet or paying extra for a roof in the galleries. That choice, a simple question of money for value received, probably explains why nobody ever complained about the weather when attending a play in the open air. It would be thought miserly to object to rain when shelter could be bought for one additional penny.

Inside the Globe's auditorium many other choices, and some conditions for which there was no choice but to submit, also offered themselves. However high the platform to which your attention is directed, in a crowd some jostling for a view is likely to be needed, especially if everyone is wearing a hat. Elizabethans all wore hats, as much indoors as out (and the Globe was a bit of both), and many hats could be an irritant to the spectators behind them. In general the higher an Elizabethan's social status the higher the hat. Apprentices and artisans, the 'rude mechanicals' of *A Midsummer Night's Dream*, wore woollen bonnets or flat caps. Court pages derisively called apprentices 'flat caps' because their own headgear was far from flat. Middle-ranked citizens, both men and women, wore felt or leather hats with a low crown and a fairly slender brim. Nobles and gentry wore high-crowned hats, usually with a bunch of feathers to increase both their height and their ability to obscure the view of anyone behind them. The most popular kind of feather was an ostrich plume. It was fortunate that at the Globe the yard was filled with flat caps, while the ostrich feathers went to the 'lords' rooms' where they obscured the view of nobody but other feather-wearers.

An equally obtrusive feature, and one which was also a mark of social divisions, was smell. The artisans carried their occupational smells with them, of course. When the tiny hall playhouse at Paul's reopened in 1599, their leading playwright hailed the fact that in its 'select' audience you need no longer expect to be 'pasted to the balmy jacket of a Beer-Brewer'.[11] More notable still, and more general, was the smell of garlic. In Elizabethan England the medicinal

*21: A woodcut from a broadside ballad, showing Elizabethan hats and fans.*

value of garlic was appreciated as much as its gastronomic value, and by folk legend it was also a safeguard against witchcraft. References to playgoing were in consequence full of complaints about the 'garlic-breathed stinkards' who flooded the yard at the amphitheatres. Out of the yard, in the twopenny galleries and lords' rooms, and especially among the stool-sitters on stage in the hall playhouses, the familiar stench was tobacco.

Tobacco was first brought to England from Virginia in 1585 or 1586. It quickly became a fashion as well as a habit. Because of the rarity and cost of the transatlantic weed the more cut-price gallants set out on a search for home-grown equivalents. Thomas Platter in 1599 reported that most gallants were smoking tobacco or 'a species of wound-wort', and claimed that 'the habit is so common with them that they always carry a pipe with them, and light up on all occasions, at a play, in a tavern or elsewhere ...'[12] John Davies sarcastically called it 'a gentleman-like smell'[13] compared with the garlic which was the other main effluent in an Elizabethan crowd.

Food and drink were available in the playhouse throughout the performance. Water was offered from leather water-bags, with pewter mugs to drink from. The water-carrier might be a would-be thespian

*22: Gallants smoking in a tavern, from a broadside ballad.*

gaining his first entry to the playhouse world, if we can judge from Sir Thomas Overbury's reference to 'a *Water-bearer* on the floore of a *Play-house*' hero-worshipping the 'wide-mouth'de *Player*' on the stage.[14] Beer was sold in bottles. There are several references to the hiss of a newly-opened bottle being misheard by the poet or player as a critical hiss from the audience. Besides drink there were apples and nuts, the apprentices often being called 'nut-crackers'. On occasions they used apple cores and nutshells to criticize the play. Overbury also refers to a law clerk eating gingerbread, and there were no doubt many other spectators who brought snacks with them to sustain them through the afternoon.

As for toilets, the evidence is regrettably negative. Even Inigo Jones's sets of plans for the Cockpit and the Court playhouse at Whitehall make no provision for that end of the chain of human needs. Playhouse owners in London did not in fact admit any responsibility for that kind of need until well into the nineteenth century.[15] There may have been buckets in the corridors at the back of the galleries. Something of the kind might be indicated by what that useful tourist Thomas Platter recorded seeing at St Paul's. The old cathedral was the most popular promenade place in London.

Booksellers' shops were lodged there, and it was the centre for all current news and gossip. So there had to be something to comfort the crowds.

Outside one of the doors there is a hewn stone, and a standard nearby where water may be obtained, and usually a bucket stands by it for passing urine, giving out a pleasant odour to the passers-by![16]

In the right-hand corner of Wenceslas Hollar's engraving of Lambeth Palace, made in the 1630s, he depicts some sheds overhanging the riverbank. These, it has been suggested, are privies.[17] Whether they were available for the general public to use, and whether there were any similar sheds on the Bankside near the Globe we do not know. Elizabethans were either very casual or very continent.

*23: The riverbank by Lambeth Palace, an engraving by Hollar. The sheds on the right overhanging the river may be privies.*

Before leaving this section about the Globe and its comforts we should also take a brief look at how the original playgoers behaved. Nobody sees a play in isolation. A crowd always has a collective personality of its own, and its mood, whether laughing or crying or objecting to what is happening on stage, is infectious. Today we usually receive Shakespeare, or indeed any play, in respectful and sometimes bored silence. Elizabethans were more active in their reactions, as you would expect when a large number of them were on their feet at the front of the auditorium. Applause in the form of clapping was commonly invited by the epilogue at the end of the play, but noises of appreciation might be offered at any time. Michael Drayton, Shakespeare's contemporary writing for the rival company, wrote of 'Shouts and Claps at ev'ry little pawse, When the proud Round on ev'ry side hath rung'.[18] Clapping and hissing or 'mewing' were instant responses, and standard audience behaviour during the play. 'The stinkards oft will hisse without a cause,/And for a bawdy jest will give applause,' wrote one unsuccessful playwright sourly in 1616.[19]

The most conspicuous audience reactions of course came from the most conspicuous playgoers, the gentlemanly gallants who sat where they could be seen, in the lords' rooms or on stools on the stage. Ben Jonson's *Every Man out of his Humour*, written in 1599 for the Globe, mocks a gallant

> Who (to be thought one of the judicious)
> Sits with his armes thus wreath'd, his hat pull'd here,
> Cryes meaw, and nods, then shakes his empty head ...[20]

And John Marston, at the Paul's playhouse in 1601, offered a similar criticism of an opinionated gallant who exercises his hostility to the playwright by snorting out during the performance, '*thats not so good, | Mew, blirt, ha ha, light Chaffy stuff* ...'[21] We know quite a lot about this form of audience behaviour, because Thomas Dekker wrote a witty satire in 1610 about how the ambitious young gallant ought to behave, including a whole chapter on the best way to act in a playhouse.

Chapter Six of *The Gull's Hornbook* is entitled 'How a Gallant should behave himself in a Play-house'. Mostly it assumes that the aspiring young fool or gull will go to an indoor playhouse and sit on the stage itself, though Dekker sometimes seems to imply that the same behaviour could be managed in an open amphitheatre. 'Let our Gallant,' he writes, presently advance himselfe up to the Throne of the Stage. I meane not into the Lords room (which is now but the Stages suburbs): No, those boxes, by the iniquity of custome, conspiracy of waiting-women and Gentlemen-Ushers, that there sweat together, and the covetousness of Sharers, are contemptibly thrust into the reare, and much new Satten is there dambd, by being smothred to death in darknesse. But on the very Rushes where the Comedy is to daunce, yea under the state of *Cambises* himselfe, must our feathered *Estridge* like a piece of Ordnance, be planted valiantly (because impudently) beating down the mewes and hisses of the opposed rascality ...

The advantages to a gull of hiring a stool and sitting on the stage to watch the play are numerous. It gives not only 'a conspicuous eminence' and 'a signed patent to engross the whole commodity of censure', but provides 'such true scenicall authority' that playwrights will flock to tell the gull about their plays before they are staged—at a tavern, and provided the gull foots the bill, of course. And to conclude, writes Dekker,

whether you be a foole, or a Justice of peace, a Cuckold, or a Capten, a Lord-Mayors sonne, or a dawcocke, a knave, or an under-Sherife; of what stamp soever you be, currant, or counterfet, the Stage, like time, will bring you to most perfect light and lay you open; neither are you to be hunted from thence, though the Scarecrows in the yard hoot at you, hisse at you, spit at you, yes, throw durt even in your teeth; 'tis most Gentlemanlike patience to endure all this, and to laugh at the silly Animals: but if the *Rabble*, with a full throat, crie away with the foole, you were worse than a madman to tarry by it: for the Gentleman and the foole should never sit on the Stage together.

From this last comment it seems that Dekker expected his gull to take the hall tradition of sitting on stools on stage to the amphitheatres. Before 1609 only the amphitheatres staged plays with fools and clowns in them, and only the amphitheatres had 'Scarecrows in the yard'. The Globe did not usually allow stools on its stage, as we know from a burlesque scene in *The Malcontent* (1604), which sends on two actors playing gallants with stools, who call for players by name to come out and talk to them—one of the actors probably called for himself to appear. They are told that it is not the Globe's practice to allow gallants on stage like this. That was part of what Dekker meant when he said a gentleman and a fool should never sit on the stage together. On the whole, at the Globe, the extremes of gallant behaviour were confined to the lords' rooms.

[68]

# 3. THE COMPANY WHICH OPERATED
# THE GLOBE

When they moved into the Globe in May 1599, Shakespeare's company had already got firm possession of their supreme asset, his plays. Even before he moved into his great decade of playwriting with *Twelfth Night* and *Hamlet* the company's plays were setting new standards of popularity, in the histories from *I Henry VI* to the Falstaff plays, in comedy with *The Taming of the Shrew* and its successors, and especially with *Romeo and Juliet*. Favourite conversation for the gentlemanly law students of the Inns of Court was quoting the plays and arguing over the merits of the leading players of the two companies.

> Luscus what's playd to day? faith now I know
> I set thy lips abroach, from whence doth flow
> Naught but pure *Juliat* and *Romeo*
> Say, who acts best? *Drusus* or *Roscio?*[23]

Even Sir John Harington, Queen Elizabeth's cousin, writing an appeal to the Lord Treasurer in 1605, spiced his letter by quoting Jaques's 'All the world's a stage' speech from *As You Like It*.[24] No playing company ever had a greater asset than this fellow-player, resident playwright and shareholder in the company.

Playing companies in Shakespeare's day were cooperatives, the eight leading players holding equal shares in the company's profits and costs. Most of Shakespeare's plays were written with not more than seven or eight major speaking parts for men. The women's parts were taken by boys, who were more or less formally bound as apprentices to particular shareholding players. With judicious doubling the plays never required more than about twenty players in all – Platter counted fifteen for *Julius Caesar*. The parts remaining after the sharers and the boys took theirs were given to 'hired men', who were not shareholders but were paid a direct wage, as were the book-holder or prompt and the stagekeepers, blue-coated assistants who carried properties on stage as required and drew back the hangings for 'discovery' scenes. Altogether the eight sharers who first occupied the Globe in 1599 (the number rose to twelve when they became the King's Men in 1603) would have employed between fifteen and twenty men and boys on a regular basis, besides some casual labour.

It was a big financial enterprise, with high profits and high risks. At any time if the number of deaths in London from plague rose above a certain figure, usually thirty in any one week, all gatherings of people, especially at playhouses, would be banned to reduce the spread of infection. The playhouses sometimes had to stay closed for more than a year when the plague was particularly bad. Usually the companies then lived off their fat years, if they had enjoyed any, and went travelling through the country with a reduced party to play in any country towns that were not bothered by the plague. Often companies broken up by this kind of trouble never reformed in London when the plague ban was lifted. Shakespeare's company was forced to travel at times, but it always renewed its London presence and ran unbroken for forty-eight years. No other company lasted more than ten, and most enjoyed no more than three years in London.

The sharers in the cooperative enterprise put an exact valuation on their shares. If a player took himself out of the company he was paid the agreed value, and a replacement sharer would have to buy his way in. Share prices were high. The Pembroke's Men to whom it is thought Shakespeare may have belonged in about 1592 valued their shares at £80 each.[25] That is rather more than Shakespeare officially paid for the second largest house in Stratford in 1597.[26] A share in the rival company to Shakespeare's in 1599 was put at £50. The value of a Chamberlain's Men's share in 1594 was probably the same.

The eight sharers of the Chamberlain's Men when it was first formed appear to have been Richard Burbage, William Shakespeare, John Heminges, William Kempe, Augustine Phillips, George Bryan, William Sly and Thomas Pope. Richard Burbage, backed by his impresario father, took the leading parts. He was the first actor to play Richard III, Hamlet, Othello and Lear. Aged about twenty-five in 1594, he outlived Shakespeare by three years and took the leading parts in the company's plays till his death. He does not seem to have been interested in the financial management of the company, which largely fell to John Heminges, a slightly older man. Heminges was married in 1588, had twelve children, one of whom became a playwright, and died in 1630 probably the wealthiest man in the company, owning a quarter of the value of both the Globe and the Blackfriars playhouses. Will Kempe was the company clown, the most famous in London from the beginning of the 1590s and in all likelihood the first player of Falstaff. Shakespeare also created Dogberry in *Much Ado* and the Nurse's man Peter in *Romeo and Juliet* for him.[27] They were all players with experience going back to the 1580s, much of an age—between Burbage's twenty-five and Shakespeare's thirty—each with distinctive talents, who evidently worked very well together. In the years from 1594 till 1600 they needed to.

24: *Will Kempe dancing a jig, from the title page of his account of his nine-day dance from London to Norwich in 1600.*

What the shares represented were partly material assets, but chiefly the collective skills of the company and its capacity to earn money by its performances. The material assets were almost entirely playbooks and costumes. Any property less portable than the costumes normally belonged to the owner of the playhouse where it would be used. Every player had his training if not his beginnings from touring plays around the country. It was common for royalty or nobility to order plays to be performed in the evenings at Court or at noblemen's houses in the Strand, to entertain the dinner guests. Plays and the properties used in them had to be portable, whether for transporting to Court or to a guildhall or marketplace in Norwich or Newcastle. It was a business involving complex teamwork, in which a single backsliding sharer could seriously embarrass his colleagues.

When a company first set up in London it almost always lacked the resources to finance itself, and had to borrow money from an impresario to get started. Travelling in the country required few plays and few costumes, because the venue was constantly changing. In London the one stable venue meant that it was the plays and properties which had to change constantly, and that was expensive. So the companies usually mortgaged their expectations of future prosperity to secure the resources which would make that prosperity possible. In London in the mid-1590s that meant using one of the two impresarios who owned playhouses and the resources that went with them. Philip Henslowe, who owned the Rose playhouse on Bankside, was one. He had come into playing through bear-baiting, and his association with playing was strengthened when his step-daughter married Edward Alleyn, the leading player of the day. Alleyn prospered so well in the Henslowe enterprises that he was able much later to found Dulwich College, known as the College of God's Gift. That foundation by a remarkable stroke of good fortune has preserved many of the Henslowe and Alleyn papers from their thirty years of involvement as London impresarios. Much of what we know about the financing of playing in Shakespeare's time comes from these papers. The other impresario, builder and owner of the Theatre playhouse in Shoreditch, was James Burbage.

Burbage is a magical name for Shakespeareans. A player himself, leader of Leicester's Men in the 1570s, James Burbage took a large hand in the three most original designs in the history of London's theatre building. The Red Lion playhouse in 1567, built by his brother-in-law John Brayne, was the first amphitheatre built exclusively for plays, with a platform stage in the yard and surrounding galleries. The Theatre, which Burbage built in 1576, was a developed version. Its timber frame was eventually pulled down and reused to

*25: Edward Alleyn, a portrait in the Dulwich Collection.*

make the Globe in 1599. And in 1596 Burbage built the Blackfriars playhouse, the most famous and successful of the hall playhouses. Almost all of Shakespeare's plays were written for one or other of Burbage's playhouses. Like Henslowe, Burbage had a family interest in the playing company he financed in 1594. As Alleyn ran his company at his father-in-law's Rose, so Burbage's son Richard ran the Chamberlain's Men at the Theatre, the Globe and eventually the Blackfriars.

Family interests, however, did not interfere with business arrangements. Alleyn's company rented the playhouse from the impresario, and paid for the playbooks, costumes and properties they used there from the daily takings. An elaborate system of loans and charges is recorded in Henslowe's diary, and carefully-worded agreements between the impresario and individual players of the company sharers are lodged in the Henslowe papers.[28] The rent for the playhouse was normally set at half the takings from the galleries, which must have been more than a third of the daily income. The precise nature of the transactions Henslowe recorded is not always easy to identify. If he paid a sharer money to release him from prison, as on occasions he had to do, it is not always clear whether humane feelings or commercial interest in regaining the services of a member of the working cooperative was guiding him. Account books rarely show the human side of such dealings. What they do show unambiguously is the complexity of the operation, the large profits that could be made when things were going well, and the gigantic appetite London was now discovering in itself for new plays and regular entertainment.

We know far less about James Burbage's enterprises than Henslowe's because his account books have not survived, and most of the evidence about him relates not to his times of prosperity but to his troubles and his brushes with the law. He built the Theatre in 1576 on land for which he took a twenty-one-year lease. Possibly he built with the thought even then in his mind that the structure might be dismantled and rebuilt elsewhere eventually. More likely, having only secured the first patent for a company to act in London two years before, he felt that the future of commercial playing was too hazardous for him to gamble more than a short lease on it. But playing did prosper, and by 1596 when the Chamberlain's Men led by his son Richard were having supreme success at the Theatre he found himself with only one year of the lease to run and an angry landlord who swore he would never allow plays to be staged there once it expired.

26. A 'View of the Cittye of London from the North towards the South', made in or before 1599. The tall structure with the flag on it is the Theatre.

What old Burbage then tried to do was quite as bold as his previous schemes, and even more brilliantly original. In October 1594 he had persuaded the Lord Chamberlain to secure permission for his company to perform at the Cross Keys Inn in Gracechurch Street, in the heart of the City. This was a special renewal of the old practice where companies managed to use City inns for playing in bad weather through the winter months. Burbage eventually wanted to renew that custom with his new company. But the Lord Mayor was hardening against it, and in the following winter he was able to impose a total ban on any performances in the City. That was when Burbage took the plunge. For £600 he bought a large hall in the liberty of the Blackfriars, and then spent a good deal more converting it into a fine indoor playhouse. He had the tradition of playing in the

[75]

City in winter on his side, and he was free of the Lord Mayor's jurisdiction because by historical accident the site of the old Blackfriars monastery, although inside the City walls below St Paul's, was a 'liberty' independent of the City authorities. As his new playhouse neared completion in 1596 Burbage thought he would be able to use it as the replacement for his twenty-year-old amphitheatre, so rescuing himself from the quarrel with the site's owner and his objection to plays. It was a radical innovation. Just as the Red Lion and the Theatre had broken new ground as playhouses built to replace the innyards and baiting houses where players had originally performed in London, so the new Blackfriars could replace the City innyards and halls which had stood in as playing places in the winter. For the first time a professional adult acting company would have a hall playhouse for their own permanent use, and it was located inside the City walls.

The plan was brilliantly clever but it failed disastrously. Blackfriars was a wealthy neighbourhood and its residents, who had tolerated the brief run by a boy company in the 1570s and 1580s in a different part of the liberty, now objected to the idea of an adult company with drums and trumpets and riotous crowds invading their privacy. A group of them presented a petition to the Privy Council asking for the scheme to be stopped. Burbage had no chance. His company's patron was himself a Blackfriars resident and signed the petition. The Lord Chamberlain, the member of the Privy Council responsible for the regulation of playgoing, was also a Blackfriars resident. Burbage died in January of the new year, leaving his sons one amphitheatre which was about to be pulled down, plus one hall playhouse which was unusable, and into which all his cash had been poured. 1597 was not a happy year for Shakespeare's company.

Burbage's elder son Cuthbert tried unsuccessfully with Richard to negotiate a new lease for the Theatre through 1597 and 1598. In July 1597 the brothers suffered another shock when the Privy Council ordered all the amphitheatres pulled down, specifying the Theatre and its Shoreditch neighbour the Curtain by name. That order was not carried out, but the Theatre's landlord, Giles Allen, had ejected his tenants by then anyway, and the company had to shift into

*27: A section of Hollar's 'Long View' of London, showing the western end of the City between St Paul's and St Bride's. The long roof below and to the right of St Bride's tall tower is probably the roof of the Blackfriars hall within which Burbage built his last playhouse.*

temporary accommodation at the Curtain and possibly the Swan. Allen intended to do away with the Theatre for his own profit – 'to convert the wood and timber thereof to some better use', as he put it a little later in a lawsuit against the Burbages.[29] He brought the lawsuit because he had been forestalled. The Burbages got in first. On 28 December 1598 they assembled at the Theatre with a master-builder and twelve workmen, watched over approvingly by the widow Burbage, to pull the playhouse down and convert its wood and timber to a better use in the shape of the Globe in Southwark.

Using the old timbers was cheaper than starting another building from scratch, but it was still very expensive. The Burbages, with most of their inheritance tied up in the empty Blackfriars playhouse, had to look elsewhere for finance. Since Richard's fellow-sharers in the Chamberlain's Men had an equal need with him for a secure playhouse it may not seem surprising that he turned to them. But it was a unique arrangement, a striking extension of the playing company's powers, and one which proved in the long run uniquely beneficial to themselves and to playgoing generally. The two Burbages between them put up half the total cost. The other fifty per cent was supplied in ten-per-cent shares by five of the other seven sharers in the company, at what must have been something like £100 per share. Shakespeare, Kempe, Heminges, Pope and Phillips were the five. Kempe left the company at the end of 1599 and his share was taken by the other four. Even then the players now had a majority control not only of the company's playing policy and its profits but also of the playhouse itself and its resources. For the first time a company was both tenant and landlord of its playhouse. That control became important ten years later when they finally secured the Blackfriars hall as old Burbage had originally planned they should back in 1596.

Between 1600 and 1608 the Burbages made some money from their father's investment by leasing the hall playhouse to a boy company for weekly performances. The boy companies, besides playing less often, claimed that their performances were 'private' while the adult companies were 'public', using the social cachet of performing for their social superiors. By so doing they eased the way for the adults to take their place once they had outstayed their welcome. Playing was banned because of plague for much of 1608, and by the time Shakespeare's company was able to begin performing at the new playhouse in 1609 they had worked out a new company system, one that once again was unique. Just as a majority of the company sharers had shares in the Globe, thereby becoming 'housekeepers', so the Burbages set up a group to share the ownership of the Blackfriars. Evidently they felt the Globe arrangement worked well. On 9 August 1608 the two Burbages, a financier called Thomas Evans, and four sharers of the King's Men signed a co-ownership document. Besides Richard Burbage the four players involved were Shakespeare, Heminges and William Sly, all Globe 'housekeepers', and Henry Condell, who had become a sharer in the company when George Bryan died and had also taken his share as a housekeeper of the Globe. Once again the players outnumbered the financiers.

Between the formulation of James Burbage's original plan to use the Blackfriars in 1596 and the first company performances in it in 1609, two things had changed. The idea of cutting in some players as playhouse owners had worked, and the playhouse they had helped to finance, the Globe, had been a success for ten years. Exactly what considerations affected the decision which was then made are not known, but since the majority of the 'housekeepers' of both playhouses were players, other factors than pure profit may well have influenced them. They decided henceforth to use the two playhouses in turn, the Globe between May and September, and the Blackfriars from October to April when the weather was bad and the hours of daylight more limited. The decision not to abandon the Globe, which old Burbage would have done, was expensive, since it meant that each playhouse was bound to stand empty for half the year.

Clearly the Globe had proved its value in the decade before 1609. If there was any doubt about that in 1608, there was none in 1613 when it burned down. The Blackfriars was on hand, and could have made a complete substitute, adequate in every respect except the sheer number of customers which the Globe's 3000 capacity and one-penny admission charge could command. The company's faith in the mass of their customers and in the Globe was reaffirmed. They rebuilt it for a price higher than any other playhouse in the whole period before 1660 is known to have cost, £1400. Such an uneconomic decision is more likely to have been made by sharers thinking as players than by housekeepers thinking as financiers.

By 1608 of course the company was as secure as any company could be in those times. King James had given them his name as their patron on 19 May 1603, within six weeks of succeeding to the throne. This was a clear advance on the other two adult companies which were then operating in London, one of which was later accorded the patronage of Prince Henry, and the other, later still, of Queen Anne. The Lord Chamberlain had retired through ill health on 6 April (he died on 9 September), but James would probably have taken the leading company under his wing in any case. The King's Men were immune from the Lord Mayor now, and retained their pre-eminence as entertainers to the Court and at the Globe for the next forty years.

# 4. PERFORMANCES AT THE GLOBE

There are many books about the staging of Shakespeare's plays. Some of them try to identify the original staging, and a few have valuable information about how particular plays were performed.[30] The subject is far too large and complex to be dealt with in this small section of this book. It would be wrong, though, not to try to give some account of the original repertory system which brought the plays to the stage, and some indication of what Shakespeare had at his disposal.

The records which John Heminges and the other sharers in Shakespeare's company kept of their business dealings have not survived. Philip Henslowe's, however, tell a graphic story of the hectic level of business which the two companies maintained through the 1590s. They kept nearly forty plays in their stock in any one year, performing them with a frequency that ranged from six times in one month to a single performance—a fate that befell nearly half the Henslowe plays. Once a playbook had been purchased by the

company, they gave themselves three weeks to bring it to performance. Each player received a 'part', his own words and cue-lines
written out for him from the playbook. The book-keeper assembled a
'plot' of the entries and exits and necessary properties, to hang in the
tiring house during the performance.

The players assembled each morning to rehearse the new plays
before launching the performance of the day at 2 pm. The sharers
regularly met with Henslowe at a tavern for their evening meal after
the show, to discuss plans and to examine new proposals for plays or
to report on new playbooks they had received (Henslowe was careful
to add the tavern bill to the list of debts the company owed him).
Casting of roles would be considered at these meetings too, and the
supply of special properties.

Casting was a fairly routine exercise, given the intensity of the
repertory system and the phenomenally rapid turnover of plays.
Kingly parts (which Shakespeare specialized in), the hero's part,
juvenile leads, the women's parts, comic old men and the clown's part
would be almost automatic assignments.[31] The theory that
individuals in the companies had standard acting 'lines' can easily be
overemphasized, but some form of typecasting would have been a
necessary simplification in a busy schedule.[32] If Richard Burbage was
assigned Richard III, Hamlet, Othello and Lear and all the other male
leads as a matter of course, a lot of time would be saved for everyone
except Burbage himself, who would have something like 800 lines a
day to memorize. Standardized acting lines for each sharer would also
simplify the job of finding a stand-in if any player fell ill, moved to
another company or died, leaving all his parts vacant.

Once the sharing system was regularized Henslowe drew up written
contracts for the players. One surviving example is worth quoting in
full because of the terms it lays down for the industrious player to
observe.

the said Robert Dawes shall and will plaie with such company, as the said Phillipp
Henslowe and Jacob Meade shall appoynte, for and during the tyme and space of
three yeares from the date hereof for and at the rate of one whole share, according
to the custome of players; and that he the said Robert Dawes shall and will at all
tymes during the said terme duly attend all suche rehearsall, which shall the night

before the rehearsall be given publickly out; and that if he the saide Robert Dawes shall at any tyme faile to come at the hower appoynted, then he shall and will pay to the said Phillipp Henslowe and Jacob Meade, their executors or assignes, Twelve pence; and if he come not before the saide rehearsall is ended, then the said Robert Dawes is contented to pay Twoe shillings; and further that if the said Robert Dawes shall not every daie, whereon any play is or ought to be played, be ready apparrelled and – to begyn the play at the hower of three of the clock in the afternoone, unless by sixe of the same company he shall be lycenced to the contrary, that then he, the saide Robert Dawes, shall and will pay unto the said Phillipp and Jacob or their assignes Three shillings; and if that he, the said Robert Dawes, happen to be overcome with drinck at the tyme when he ought to play, by the judgement of ffower of the said company, he shal and will pay Tenne shillings; and if he shall faile to come during any plaie, having noe lycence or just excuse of sicknes, he is contented to pay Twenty shillings. And further the said Robert Dawes doth covenant ... that if he shall at any time after the play is ended depart or goe out of the playhowse with any playhouse apparell on his body, ... or shal be consenting or privy to any other of the said company going out of the howse with any of their apparell on his or their bodies, he, the said Robert Dawes, shall and will forfeit and pay unto the said Phillip and Jacob, or their administrators or assignes, the some of ffortie pounds of lawfull money.[33]

Missing rehearsals or being drunk on duty was bad enough, but the real crime was stealing company costumes.

With a different play every day, and no guarantee that a new play would enjoy more than the one performance, there was little reason to build elaborate sets or properties. The company in any case had to be mobile enough to make the journey from the afternoon's perform-ance at the Globe to an evening at Court or elsewhere on the affluent side of the City. The scenery was largely composed of the hangings across the entry doors in the back wall of the stage platform, and of the costumes. Few heavy properties other than a curtained bed, a throne on a dais, a banquet table and stools or benches are needed in Shakespeare's plays. This limited resource, indicating localities by emblems or words (both easily portable) or leaving the scene unlocalized, was one of the necessary enabling features of Shakespearean staging. It guaranteed a fast, direct, economical and easily transportable performance. Audiences did not regret the absence of scenery because most of them had never seen any. Not until Court masques, with their marvellous tricks of perspective scenery contrived by Inigo Jones, had become the standard criterion of courtiers under Charles in the 1630s was there any attempt to put

# The platt of The Seccound parte of the Seuen Deadlie Sinns

28: Part of the 'plot' hung up in the tiring house for a play at Philip Henslowe's Rose playhouse. The square hole in the centre is for the peg on which the board holding the 'plot' was hung.

*29: A vignette from the title page of Nathanael Richards'* Messallina, *1640, showing the stage of a hall playhouse with its stage hangings.*

scenery on the common stages, and it was rarely done even then. Emblematic staging began with the hangings which spread across the tiring-house wall. In *A Warning for Fair Women* (1599), a Chamberlain's company play, the Induction which begins the play has History, Comedy and Tragedy each objecting to the other fashions in plays. Tragedy wins when Comedy realizes that 'the stage is hung with blacke; and I perceive / The Auditors preparde for *Tragedie*'.[34] It was evidently standard practice to advertise the nature of the play, whether tragedy or comedy, in the colour of the hangings so that anyone who had not registered the subject on the playbill would be properly prepared. A drawing of stage hangings for a hall-playhouse play of the 1630s shows a rather adolescent Cupid with bow drawn.[35] Presumably that was for romantic comedy. Clowns used the hangings for their comic entrances, in the fashion still to be found with stand-up comics. Two anecdotes about Richard Tarlton, the first great stage clown of the 1580s, say that he only had to peep out through the hangings to start the audience laughing. Praise for the identical trick was given to the clown at Salisbury Court playhouse in the 1630s.[36]

Once the play was under way localities were indicated emblematically. For scenes at Court or trial scenes in courtrooms a throne or 'chair of judgement' or 'chair of state', raised on a dais, would dominate the stage platform and signify the type of place for the scene. The king or judge would sit on it as the natural focus of attention and authority, while around him the courtiers and courtroom attendants would remove their hats in token of his authority. In the presence of a king they would kneel before speaking. Sir Thomas Smith's *De Republica Anglorum*, published in 1583, states unequivocally that 'no man speaketh to the prince nor serveth at the table but in adoration and kneeling, all persons of the realme be bareheaded before him, insomuch that in the chamber of presence, where the cloath of estate is set, no man dare walke, yea though the prince be not there, no man dare tarrie there but bareheaded.'[37] The 'cloth of estate' was the tapestry with the royal arms on it which hung behind the chair of state. Smith's statement reminds us that thrones and crowns were very tangible emblems of authority in Elizabethan times. They dictated forms of respect that nobody dared to flout. Hamlet's behaviour to King Claudius on his throne was much more shocking in 1600 than it can be made today.

Kings and princes appeared on Shakespeare's stage nearly as often in battles as they did on the throne at Court. Battles needed no particular indication of locality as a rule, only the processional entry of troops armed with swords and pikes led by a drummer and an ensign

[85]

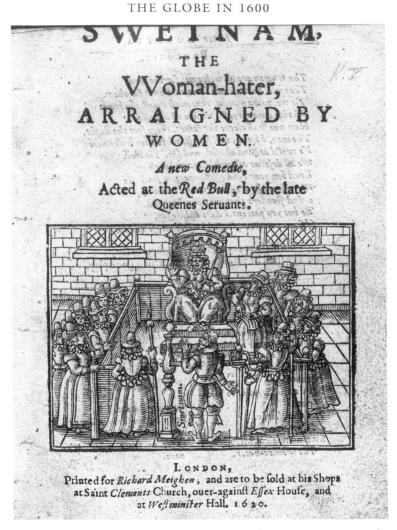

SWETNAM,

THE

VVoman-hater,

ARRAIGNED BY

WOMEN.

*A new Comedie,*

Acted at the *Red Bull*, by the late
Queenes Seruants.

LONDON,

Printed for *Richard Meighen*, and are to be sold at his Shops
at Saint *Clements* Church, ouer-againſt *Eſſex* Houſe, and
at *Weſtminſter* Hall. 1620.

*30: The title page of an anonymous play,* Swetnam the Woman Hater, *performed at the Red Bull in 1619. The chair on which the woman judge sits is the kind of throne used on stage for scenes at the Court and courtroom scenes.*

with his banner. Actual battles usually seem to have involved a lot of coming and going, single-sword combats, and the sounds of trumpet-calls and drums offstage. Trumpets and drums were the normal means of transmitting orders on the battlefield in Elizabethan armies. Every playgoer knew the call for a charge or a retreat, and the 'flourish'

[86]

*31: George Gascoigne presenting his book to Queen Elizabeth. Her throne with its cloth of estate and canopy was the standard equipment for the royal 'presence'.*

which announced a victorious or ceremonial entry. Sometimes guns might be fired, onstage or off, to add to the uproar. An account in a letter of 1586 tells of the accidental discharge of a real bullet, probably at Henslowe's playhouse in a performance of Marlowe's *2 Tamburlaine*, which 'killed a chyld, and a woman great with chyld'.[38] Onstage swordfighting was extremely popular, always in the form of

[87]

single-sword duels. Some players were highly skilled fencers, though their skill did not prevent an accident in 1622 when an apprentice sitting on the edge of an amphitheatre platform was injured by a player's sword. The apprentice entered the spirit of the occasion by promptly challenging the player to a duel.[39] In one play of Shakespeare's a battle was given a locality identified by a signboard, but that was for a special reason: in *2 Henry VI* Somerset is given a prophecy that he will die before a castle, and the prophecy is ironically fulfilled when he is killed under the signboard of the Castle tavern in St Albans. Evidently the company hung up an inn sign for the purpose.[40]

The more domestic scenes were also indicated by emblems. Tables and benches were provided for banquets, as in *Macbeth* and *As You Like It*. An equally functional emblem was the canopied bed put out for bedroom scenes, such as the one which concludes *Othello* with husband and wife both lying dead on the bed. Of course costuming could easily stand in when the bed itself was not needed. Nightcaps and nightgowns were an entirely adequate means of conveying sleep-time scenes, especially when the nightcap wearer entered with a candle in his or her hand. Candles or torches (burning faggots of reeds or wood) were brought on stage to mark night scenes, since the open-air stage had no means of dimming the sun. Costumes were one of the commonest ways of signifying changes of locality, time or action. Just as chest-armour showed readiness for battle, so night attire showed nighttime, and a cloak marked an outdoor scene. Riding boots and cloak indicated travel. *Look About You*, a Henslowe play of 1600, opens with Robin Hood and a servant entering '*with ryding wandes in theyr handes as if they had beene new lighted*'. Horses did not appear on stage, so journeys began and ended offstage with characters entering as if they had just dismounted, or leaving as if about to leap on their horses. A play staged in about 1615 has a character enter after a great crash is heard offstage, all muddied and cursing his horse which he says has just fallen.

One special kind of entry is important because it has caused a lot of confusion about whether the Globe had an 'inner stage', the small picture-frame stage in the wall at the back of the stage platform whose existence was taken for granted for many years. There is no evidence that the Globe did have such a secondary stage area, but it did have an alcove or 'discovery space' for small set-piece displays which could offer the nearest thing to scenic staging Shakespeare ever used. A study or monastic cell would be exposed by drawing back the stage hangings, to show (usually) a solitary figure seated at a table with book and candle. It was a small space, and often supplied a 'show' without any figure in it, like the pile of treasure at the beginning of *Volpone*. If a figure was revealed, he promptly moved forward onto the stage platform. Shakespeare's two most famous 'discoveries' made special use of the Elizabethan tradition of using 'discoveries' as part of a funeral monument. Statues of the memorial figure, modelled in painted terracotta or alabaster, were often shown kneeling in prayer or lying in state behind a curtain drawn back to show the statue to the observer. The curtains represented the figure's privacy, as it might be 'discovered' at its normal and private devotions. Shakespeare used this funerary 'discovery' in his last two plays, both of which end with a scene in which a figure thought to be dead is 'discovered' and then brought to life.[41] In *The Winter's Tale* Hermione's statue is a perfect funeral monument discovered to King Leontes by the attendant Paulina, which then comes to life when Paulina summons it with music. In *The Tempest* a less miraculous and more neatly comic discovery is revealed to King Alonso when Prospero draws back the hangings to show Ferdinand and Miranda, the son whom Alonso thought dead, and the daughter whom Prospero has just declared he has lost. The pair discovered together might well have been caught behaving very differently, but they are playing at chess.

Such discovery scenes were special and infrequent set pieces in Shakespeare's plays. A much more common use of the discovery space's hangings was for simple concealment and eavesdropping. Jonson's *Volpone*, written for the Globe in 1605, besides opening with the 'discovery' of Volpone's hoard, has several scenes later where Volpone stands on a stool to peep over the hangings and watch his victims make fools of themselves. The same hangings conceal Polonius when he eavesdrops on Hamlet in Gertrude's bedroom and is killed when Hamlet's sword plunges through '*the arras*'. If the player of Polonius stood well back in the discovery space he had room to wait till he saw the sword cut through before falling heavily to the ground, when Hamlet would draw back the hangings to 'discover' the corpse.

From murder to music is a long step, but many of the plays had as much or more of the one than the other. Songs are present in most of the comedies, and were usually accompanied by instruments. Some were as portable as the costumes, in the earlier years. The singer might accompany himself on the lute or with the pipe and small side-drum that country clowns used. Recorders and viols or other strings were also used in some plays, besides the trumpets and drums of martial music in plays like *Henry V*, which has many references to the concord of martial music in its verse images. Until about 1608 the instrumental music at the Globe seems to have been either onstage or played '*within*', in the discovery space behind the hangings.[42] The 1604 Induction to *The Malcontent* at the Globe speaks of the 'not received custome of musick at our Theater'. In saying that, though, the player was contrasting his company's practices with those of the boy companies in the halls. At the Blackfriars the boys were accompanied by a famous consort of musicians who gave an hour's concert as an overture before the play, as well as playing at each pause between the acts and accompanying the songs. Shakespeare's company did not make pauses between the acts as a rule, but when they took over the Blackfriars they started to do so, and that may reflect their acquisition of the Blackfriars musicians along with the playhouse. They seem also to have adapted one of the lords' rooms on the balcony at the Globe into a curtained-off music room. *The Tempest* is a play rich with instrumental music as well as songs, and seems to acknowledge the acquisition of an enhanced musical resource ripe for exploitation.

Much more could be said about the original staging at the Globe. These short examples, though, may serve as a general introduction and a sign of how distinct an experience playgoing was in Shakespeare's time compared with what we expect today. Only two more points need to be made before we can turn to the material facts about the Globe's design. First, plays in Shakespeare's day were more than just an entertainment or 'distraction' as the theatre is in our day. In the absence of newspapers, or any other media for publishing opinions and registering the talking-points of daily news, plays became daily currency and a means of exchange for the talk of the town. Everything we might expect to find in today's newspapers, from domestic murder stories to yesterday's battle across the Channel, were taken as currency for London's playhouses. Players and their playwrights were eager to make use of current affairs, an enthusiasm which provoked censorship on the one hand and violent audience reactions on the other. All the classical subjects for gossip – sex, religion and politics – were broached either directly or covertly in the plays of the time.[43] And secondly, these mass reactions evoked intense and potent emotions. Amphitheatres and plays were enough of a novelty in London in the 1590s for the novelty itself to generate excitement. Never before, even in churches, had thousands of people gathered together to respond collectively to the topics of the day set out in emotive fictions. Patriotism was one mass emotion, for instance, that the war plays of the 1590s exploited in a decade when England was fighting a sharp religious and political war against the Spanish in the Netherlands. Thomas Nashe acclaimed Shakespeare's *I Henry VI* as the most popular play of the time, when he wrote, in 1592,

How would it have joyed brave *Talbot* (the terror of the French) to thinke that after hee had lyne two hundred yeares in his Tombe, hee should triumphe againe on the Stage, and have his bones newe embalmed with the teares of ten thousand spectators at the least, (at severall times) who, in the Tragedian that represents his person, imagine they behold him fresh bleeding![44]

Perhaps the most vivid testimony to the emotion-swaying power of Shakespeare's company appeared in a report by an Oxford don in 1610, praising (in Latin) their performance of *Othello* at the university. The pathos focused on the boy playing Desdemona, motionless and speechless on the bed at the end of the play:

Not only by their speaking but by their acting they drew tears – indeed Desdemona, killed by her husband, although she always acted the matter very well, in her death moved us even more greatly, when lying in bed she implored the pity of the spectators with her face alone.[45]

[91]

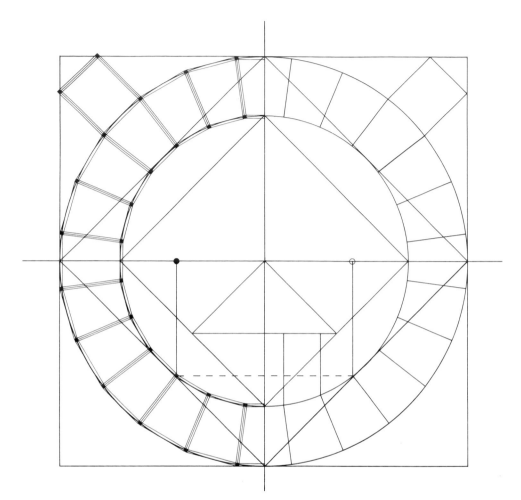

*32: Setting-out diagram for the new Globe, showing the layout of the stage within the circle of galleries, including the external stair turrets. Theo Crosby's architect's drawing.*

# CHAPTER 3

# THE ORIGINAL GLOBE

## by John Orrell

On St Peter's Day, 30 June 1613, the first Globe theatre was consumed by fire. The King's Men, led by Richard Burbage, were in the midst of a performance of Shakespeare's latest play, *Henry VIII*, spectacular in their embroidered costumes as they trod the matted stage. The moment came when Henry makes his menacing surprise visit to Wolsey's household at York Place. The text calls for '*Drum and trumpet. Chambers discharged*', a 'warlike voice' to announce the arrival of 'a noble troop of strangers'. On the fatal day, however, the voice of the chambers, or cannon, accompanied a tongue of fire which accidentally caught the thatch. The wind rapidly fanned the flames all around the roof, and in an hour or two the house was in ruins, though no one was hurt beyond one man whose flaming breeches were doused with bottle ale.

Sir Henry Wotton, whose letter to a nephew is the most detailed contemporary description of the fire, lamented the ruin of what he called 'that virtuous fabric', though it seems that he thought its virtue one of association rather than architectural or material value. 'Nothing did perish,' he observed, 'but wood and straw,' and other commentators struck a similar note. Ben Jonson, for example, acknowledged that the Globe was 'the glory of the Bank', but likened it to a moated fort – presumably one of the Tudor coastal castles like Deal or Walmer – 'flanked with a ditch, and forced out of a marish [marsh]'. A poetic boatman turned the affair into a lubberly epigram:

As gold is better that's in fier try'd,
So is the Bank-side *Globe*, that late was burn'd;
For where before it had a thatched hide,

[93]

# THE ORIGINAL GLOBE

Now to a stately theator 'tis turn'd
Which is an emblem, that great things are won
By those that dare through greatest dangers run.[1]

There may indeed have been an element of daring in the King's Men's determination to rebuild. Using the old foundation – as contemporary building regulations required them to do – they soon remade the theatre, but at an expense considerably greater than the original. Later estimates agree that they spent about £1400 on the replacement, which was according to one report 'new builded in far fairer manner than before', and according to another 'the fairest that ever was in England'.[2] There seems to be no doubt, then, that the second Globe was a more beautiful structure than the first, and more expensive despite the fact that it was no bigger in plan and may even have been built of inferior materials. According to a survey of 1634, made to identify which buildings in Southwark were of brick and which of timber, and to list those illegally constructed on new foundations, the Globe was 'built with timber, about 20 yeares past, upon an old foundation'.[3] In the same year the Globe's timbers also happened to be mentioned in a lawsuit concerning the lease of the theatre. A carpenter, questioned about the scrap value of the materials in the event that the structure were torn down, replied that they might be worth only £200:

the said materialls ... wilbee shorte it beinge the most parte ffur Tymber, and the lead thereof very thynne ...

Another witness deposed that the playhouse was built 'with old Pollard' which 'will not bee so usefull as younger tymber is'.[4] Whatever 'old Pollard' may be, the second Globe was mostly built of fir, a timber imported from the Baltic and cheaper than native oak. The stately theatre, the fairest that ever was in England, was made of second-rate stuff; much of the great cost of its construction must have gone into workmanship and expensive decoration.

Possibly some of the 'old Pollard' was timber recovered from the fire of 1613. Anyone who has seen a burnt-out Tudor frame building will remember the way the great hardened posts and beams survive the catastrophe, charred but largely unconsumed. Contemporary witnesses say that the Globe burned away entirely ('consuming ... the

[94]

whole house to the very grounds,' said Wotton; and John Chamberlain wrote that it 'burn'd ... down to the ground'), but it is hard to believe that none of the massive timbers survived to be incorporated in the rebuilding.

Those timbers had a long history which began in 1576 when James Burbage and his brother-in-law John Brayne joined forces to construct a playhouse not far from the city walls in Shoreditch. Brayne had already been responsible nine years before for setting up London's earliest purpose-built playhouse in the garden of a farmhouse called the Red Lion in Whitechapel. The galleries, courtyard and stage which he commissioned then will doubtless have suggested the design of the Shoreditch enterprise, which the entrepreneurs called very simply by the direct Roman name: the Theatre.[5] This building, constructed on a plot with a twenty-one-year lease, was used by various companies of players, the latest of whom were the Lord Chamberlain's Men. When the ground lease ran out in 1597 the players left the Theatre and transferred to the neighbouring Curtain, a similar house which had been constructed some twenty years before. James Burbage having died early that year, his son Cuthbert pursued negotiations with the landlord for a renewal of the lease at the Theatre, but with little success. In the end, taking careful note that the original lease included a covenant permitting the tenant to pull down and remove the playhouse on expiry, Cuthbert employed a carpenter, Peter Street, to supervise its methodical demolition, an event which began in December 1598.

The landlord, Giles Allen, got wind of this enterprise too late to prevent it, but soon took the usual Elizabethan route of pursuing the matter in court. Meanwhile Peter Street had packed the timbers of the Theatre off to Bankside, where he set about re-erecting them as the Globe. Nothing in the mass of legal documents which later emerged to chronicle this event gives any detailed idea of the timbers themselves, their nature and specifications, but they will have consisted of large, valuable pieces of oak, carefully cut into the complex joints by means of which they could be pegged together.[6] There will have been vertical posts and the horizontal groundsills into which they were inserted. The upper horizontal members were called

[95]

bressummers, and these will have been accompanied with the usual joists, 'prick posts' (or intermediate vertical timbers of smaller dimension), rafters, purlins, etc. An Elizabethan timber frame made of such units could be dismantled much as it had been assembled in the first place, almost like a Meccano set, with the difference that because the joints were all uniquely cut the individual members were not interchangeable. Consequently they were marked close to the joints with matching incisions, often Roman numerals or rune-like slashes, so that the correct mortise could be brought to the appropriate tenon. When Peter Street was interrupted by one of Allen's minions in the course of pulling down the Theatre, he fobbed the man off with a claim that he was dismantling the frame in order to set it up again on the same site, but in a different form.[7] The ruse apparently worked well enough to buy Street the time he needed, and the fact that it did so testifies to the care with which he was proceeding: Allen's servant could see that the timbers were being taken apart in such a way that they could be reused.

Street did not intend to put the timbers together again in a new form, but on a new site, a plot of ground to the south of Maid Lane on Bankside. The lease was for thirty-one years from Christmas 1598, and – as we have seen – was entered into by a syndicate representing the Lord Chamberlain's Men. Where the Theatre had belonged to James Burbage and John Brayne alone, the new Globe was shared among the principals of the acting company.[8] It may be that the Burbages, whose fortunes had been diminished by their father's recent undertaking to construct an indoor playhouse at the Blackfriars, were forced to such cooperative financing by economic necessity. They contributed the used timbers from the Theatre, a form of capital investment that earned Cuthbert and his brother Richard a half-share in the new house, and the fact that the building was thatched where it might more safely have been tiled perhaps suggests that it was underfunded. Nevertheless the novel mode of proprietorship was to have an important influence on the nature of the theatrical enterprise that flourished within its walls.

For thirteen years, then, getting on for fourteen, the first Globe stood on Bankside like a Tudor fort before succumbing to its own fire. From those years no detailed drawing of it survives, no adequate ground plan, no minute description. We do not have a copy of the builder's contract, nor does it appear on an estate survey. The tally of documents relating to it is by no means a short one – in fact both the Theatre and the Globe were the subjects of much litigation and therefore of court reporting – but little enough in the papers describes the physical structure of the playhouses. Unfortunately, therefore, the reconstruction of the Globe cannot proceed directly from a vast data base, like that which informs the rebuilt Williamsburg. It is a matter of diligent, patient and above all cooperative enquiry.

The serious study of Elizabethan playhouses that was undertaken in the latter part of the nineteenth century and much developed in the twentieth has been reviewed in Chapter One. New evidence continues to emerge – for example in the documents concerning the Boar's Head theatre in Whitechapel discovered by Leslie Hotson and C.J. Sisson and now admirably interpreted by Herbert Berry – and on the whole it confirms the findings of scholars such as Reynolds and Hosley.[9] Yet despite the steady accumulation of facts and their methodical reassessment we are still unable to offer anything like a definitive design for the first Globe. In particular we have had little architectural sense of the building, the result perhaps of its study having generally been the province of literary rather than architectural historians. Yet in order to begin the reconstruction on Bankside we have had to determine the shape, the proportions, the size and the orientation of the main frame of the theatre, even before passing on to determine such matters as the stage roof or the number of stage entrances. Most theatre studies have concentrated quite properly on the interior of the house; but as rebuilders we have had first to determine its ground plan.

Several pictures of the first Globe do survive, and show it as either round or polygonal in plan, so that we do have at least a minimal idea of what type of structure it was. The two earliest of these depictions are also the most authoritative. They both appear on the same set of sheets, a four-plate panorama of London prepared by the professional surveyor John Norden in 1600 – very soon, that is, after the Globe first appeared among the rooftops of Bankside. In the view itself,

*33: A detail from the panorama of London by John Norden, made in 1600.*

engraved from Norden's original, the roof of the Globe may just be spotted emerging from the treetops at the edge of one of the sheets. Close by is the Rose, which may be discerned rather more easily; to the west rises the profile of the Bear Garden, and upriver we can see the Swan. All this is perfectly correct for the year 1600: Norden shows exactly the playhouses we know to have been standing at that time, and gives them, as far as may be judged, in their correct positions. Each is rendered as polygonal in plan, the Globe and Rose apparently hexagonal and the Swan and Bear Garden octagonal. But in a map inset to one side of the view the Bankside area appears again. The map itself is a revision of Norden's earlier one of 1593, which had shown – as was correct for the time – only the Rose and the Bear Garden (labelled 'The play howse' and 'The Beare howse'). Now, bringing his old map up to date, Norden adds the Swan in the correct location; he retains the 'Bearegarden' and the Rose (miscalling it 'The stare'), and adds 'The globe', all positioned in relation to each other almost exactly as in the panorama. Each house bears a flag, and the

[98]

*34: The 'inset' from Norden's panorama of 1600.*

Globe is unmistakably given a thatched roof where the others have tile. But in this case all the playhouses are shown as round in plan.[10]

Round or polygonal? The most authoritative views of the first Globe tell us both. Nevertheless if we are to rebuild the structure on Bankside we must answer the question one way or another. It is the sort of imperative that will not brook compromise. Other images of the theatre are not much help. John Speed's atlas, the *Theatre of the Empire of Great Britain* (1611–12), contains a small inset panorama of London by Jodocus Hondius dated 1610, in which the Globe is reported to be circular, with a curious lean-to ambulatory running round its lower storey. Here the Bear Garden is polygonal, as it is in the background of an engraved equestrian portrait of James I by Francis Delaram.[11] But this is merely based on Hondius. A far more influential picture of the theatres was printed in the beautiful panorama of London by Claes Jan Visscher, published in Amsterdam in or before 1616. Here we are shown the Swan, 'The Bear Gardne' and the Globe, all beflagged polygonal structures almost as tall as they

*Plate III: The Globe as it might have been in 1599. A view of the stage from the top gallery.*

*See note on p. 181.*

are wide.[12] Because the view shows London as it was some years earlier it has generally been assumed that the Globe is the first theatre of that name and not the second, despite the fact that the fire and rebuilding had taken place well before the date inscribed on the extant prints. Perhaps because of its singular beauty, the panorama has had an astonishing influence over the imaginations of scholars of the Shakespearean theatre. In the nineteenth century it formed the basis of countless redrawn pictures of the Globe, and in the twentieth it significantly shaped the reconstructions of J. Cranford Adams and Irwin Smith. Yet its presentation of the Bankside area appears to be merely a restatement in perspective of the topographical facts contained in an atlas map of London that had been published in Cologne in 1572. This was in turn copied from a lost copperplate map of *c.* 1560, long before the arrival of the theatres on Bankside.[13] Where the old map offered bull-baiting and bear-baiting arenas close to some schematized rectangular fishponds, Visscher merely inserted his Bear Garden and Globe, retaining most of the other ancient (and by 1616 inaccurate) features of the landscape. The greater part of Visscher's view concerns the north bank of the river, and in 1948 I. A. Shapiro conclusively demonstrated that his source here was Norden's panorama of 1600.[14] There is no reliable evidence that Visscher ever set foot in London: if his Globe, Bear Garden and Swan are polygonal it is merely because he saw them as polygonal in his source, on which he relied so fully as to redraw the round baiting arenas of the atlas with angled structures evidently based on Norden's representation of the Swan.[15] It appears that his view has no independent authority whatever, and it should be categorically dismissed as evidence on which to base a reconstruction of the Globe.

Without doubt Norden is the best qualified witness of the Bankside theatres in the period of the first Globe. He was a geometer, a practising surveyor and mapmaker, a disciplined observer of the scene. In the panorama he is shown at the top of St Saviour's tower (now Southwark Cathedral), gazing out at the view beneath the tag 'Statio prospectiva', a tiny figure in a great shady hat, his right arm holding aloft a pair of surveyor's compasses. If we are to trust anyone's picture of the first Globe, it must be his. Yet while his view

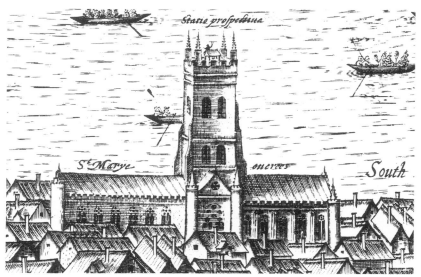

*35: Norden at his 'station point' on the top of St Saviour's church (now Southwark Cathedral), holding up a pair of surveyor's compasses.*

to the north of the river is essentially just what would be seen from the church tower–so that Guildhall, for example, exactly aligns with Coldharbour, and St Paul's appears just to the right of Queenhythe, all precisely as they could be seen from St Saviour's–the representation of the south bank is not. By including the point of view itself, what theorists call the 'station point', Norden was creating an artificial composition and therefore offering an imaginary bird's-eye view of the church, of Winchester House nearby, and of all the theatres including the Globe. Nevertheless his was an informed imagination, one based–as Visscher's was not–on first-hand observation, not merely on previous published sources. In fact Norden's Bankside appears to be a translation into perspective form of the plan of the area given in his map, the roads and riverbank tracing almost identical patterns in both. The Bear Garden is set in the view in elevation, as if seen from the side, while the nearby Rose and Globe are shown as seen from above. I think it likely that both are the products of rough sketches taken from the 'statio prospectiva' of the church tower, with whose elevated sightlines they are nicely consistent.

Yet it is Norden himself who clouds the issue by showing the Globe both round (in the inset map) and polygonal (in the panorama). In order to clarify matters we have to turn to a variety of other evidence, including first principles. We know that the frame was constructed from timber, and it is not in the nature of such construction to produce buildings which are perfectly circular in plan. The frame is made of vertical posts supporting horizontal bressumers and joists. If the horizontal members are anything but straight their own weight —let alone any load they may be required to bear—will exert torsion on the joints with the posts, and the structure will be unstable.[16] A timber-frame structure must therefore have straight walls, although it is not impossible that they might be faked up with falsework to look curved if required. But we have reason to believe that the first Globe was not a lavish building, and such expenditures on the exterior would have been an unproductive use of the sharers' money.

The Globe's timber frame was that of the Shoreditch Theatre transposed to the new site, and it happens that we have an engraving of that earlier playhouse. At the university library in Utrecht is an unique copy of 'The View of the City of London from the North to the South', made probably at some time in the 1590s and engraved quite possibly by the same hand as was employed for Norden's panorama. To the extreme left of the view a theatre may be seen, topped by a flag. A little to the right a similar flag rises above some intervening rooftops, and its appears that the artist has registered the Theatre (to the left) and the neighbouring Curtain.[17] This depiction of the Theatre shows it taller than it is wide, much like Norden's Swan; and it is unmistakably polygonal—perhaps octagonal—with attached wings to either side, presumably staircase turrets.

Yet if we can look back to the Theatre for confirmation of the view that the Globe was polygonal, we can look forward to the second Globe, built on the same foundations as the first and therefore identical in plan, to find that it was apparently round. The finest panorama of seventeenth-century London is that of Wenceslas Hollar, etched in Antwerp in 1647. It shows the second Globe and the Bear Garden (by now reconstructed as the Hope), but with their labels accidentally transposed. Both are, however, clearly rendered as circular buildings. Moreover we have two preliminary sketches of the theatres from Hollar's hand. One – the more cursory of the two – is an imaginary bird's-eye sketch, part of a single panoramic sweep perhaps intended as a compositional exercise in preparation for the great etching. It shows the Hope and Globe without indicating any polygonal faces. The other drawing is much more detailed and is evidently a precise eyewitness study made from the top of St Saviour's tower. It appears to be the chief basis for the west Southwark part of the etching itself, and as a drawing made on the spot it has the prior claim to our attention. This is, surely, the finest piece of visual evidence about the Globe, and its gives no hint of a polygonal frame.[18]

We are, I think, close to the point where we can reach a conclusion about this awkward question. But before we do so we should notice two more pieces of evidence. The first is a drawing of the Swan theatre originally made *c.* 1596 by a visiting Dutch traveller, Johannes de Witt, and surviving only in a copy made by his friend Aernout van Buchell. With it is a brief account, in Latin, of the playhouses that de Witt had seen on his visit to London.[19] The sketch shows the inside of the Swan as round in plan, apparently with curved horizontal bressummers between the posts. In the accompanying narrative de Witt observes that London boasts four such 'amphitheatres' – he means the Theatre, the Curtain, the Rose and the Swan – of which the Swan is the largest and most distinguished. It reminds him of Roman work, and in that spirit he labels its parts in his drawing with Latin names drawn mostly from the ancient theatre. And he observes that the house was 'constructum ex coaceruato lapide pyrritide': made of a concrete of flintstones. Such construction is, as he says, common in parts of Britain, and it would permit the incorporation of a round plan. But a second piece of evidence seems to contradict de Witt. In 1613 Philip Henslowe contracted with a carpenter for the construction of the Hope theatre, the same one as is shown in the Hollar drawings. There is no doubt that this was a wooden frame, for the extant contract usefully tells us the precise dimensions of the timbers, specifically mentioning that cheaper fir might be used for 'the vpright postes on the backparte of the . . . stories'; but it also tells us that the

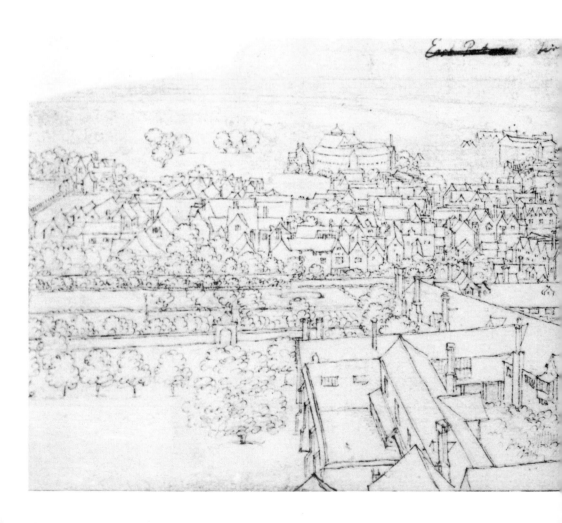

36: Hollar's panorama of 1647.
Above: A sketch showing the theatres.
Below: The detailed drawing for the Southwark area of the panorama.
Opposite: A detail of the complete panorama.

Convent garden.    S. Clement

Arundel house
Glas house
Temple stayrs
Temple
Black fryars
Baynards Castle

The Globe

Beere bayting

Southwark toward Westminster

timber Hope was to be built 'of suche large compasse, fforme, widenes, and height as the Plaie howse Called the Swan'. And again, the Hope was 'to be made in althinges and in suche forme and fashion, as the saide plaie house called the swan (the scantling of the tymbers, tyles, and foundacion as ys aforesaide without fraude or coven)'. [20] This contractual evidence surely overrides de Witt's touristic observations, and we may conclude that both the Swan and the Hope were made of timber, though doubtless rendered on the outside with lime and hair sufficiently to have deceived the visitor's eye.

Our best witnesses seem to contradict each other. Nevertheless a solution is not far away. The Globe's frame was made of timbers and therefore must have been polygonal. It could have been dressed up to look round, but only at pointless expense. Norden shows it as both polygonal and round, and the most reasonable conclusion is that its plan was a polygon that posed as a circle, with many sides rather than few. Norden and the author of the view of London from the north showed the theatres with few sides because of the small scale at which they were working: their little pictures were topographers' simplifications, just as Norden's map offered the cartographer's half-symbolic simplification of the circle. Hollar likewise declined to record the theatres' angled faces, perhaps because he acknowledged that they were essentially circles in any case. As to the number of sides, apart from the argument that they were many rather than few, I must postpone discussion until we have considered the proportions of the ground plan of the structure.

The enquiry into the shape of the Globe, though obviously necessary, is too long for comfort. It has, however, introduced a mass of evidence to which we can now refer more briefly, but there remains one document of prime importance that has so far gone unmentioned. That is the builder's contract for the Fortune playhouse, constructed by Peter Street for Philip Henslowe soon after the first Globe had opened. Henslowe, probably deeming it wise to move well away from such weighty competition, established his new playhouse north of the city close to Whitecross Street beyond Cripplegate. Here the Lord Admiral's Men duly transferred from the

Rose, the Globe's close neighbour, in the autumn of 1600. The Fortune was different from the other theatres in that it had a square plan, and like the Rose it was somewhat smaller than the Swan and the Globe. But it was built by the same Peter Street who had supervised the dismantling of the Theatre and who had presumably gone on to reassemble it as the Globe, and in the contract there is constant if tantalizingly unspecific reference to the Globe as the exact model to be followed in such matters as the staircases, the access passages, the divisions of the galleries, the design of the stage and many other details.[21] The main differences, mentioned or implied, appear to have been that the Fortune was square in plan and made of timbers of larger dimension, its roof was tiled where the model's was thatched, and it was adorned within with square-sectioned posts carved as satyrs, where the Globe presumably had turned columns.

This contract, like de Witt's sketch of the Swan, is a rich source of information, and we shall return to it later. Our present concern is with the Globe's ground plan, and here the Fortune is relevant to our purposes, though because of its square shape its relevance is indirect. Peter Street was an Elizabethan carpenter, a substantial man but illiterate, able only to set his mark to the document. His methods would be those he learned during his apprenticeship, passed on by word of mouth and by example, not through the medium of books. Furthermore his measuring instruments, though they included a carpenter's 10-foot 'yard' or stick and a surveyor's line marked off at intervals of one rod or perch (16 feet 6 inches), did not in his day extend to a calibrated measuring tape, the invention of a later age. The *decempeda*, together with a carpenter's square and some lines and pegs, would be perfectly adequate for setting out the square plan of the Fortune, 80 feet each way according to the contract, and with a square yard within it measuring 55 feet each way. But these instruments could help him with a polygonal plan of the sort used at the Globe only if they were deployed according to systems of geometrical construction which were in fact the common inheritance of medieval artisans, especially of masons and carpenters. Such procedures were not merely one way of doing things among others, any of which Street could pull at will from his bag of tricks; rather they constituted a quite fundamental predisposition towards the geometrical method of deciding on the proportions of a building.

A recent study of Street's method at the Fortune shows that the plan of the frame, together with the 43-foot width of the stage set up within it, could have been laid out by means of a standard 3-rod surveyor's line deployed according to venerable *ad triangulum* and *ad quadratum* techniques which made use of the line to mark out equilateral triangles and squares on the ground.[22] Street will have thought of his timber frame in terms of the intervals between post centres, rather than in the superficial 'lawfull assize' of the contract. Considered thus, the conceptual lines of the frame—and the centre lines of the brick foundation walls beneath it—were laid out *ad quadratum*, the diagonals of the yard being equal to the sides of the outer wall. Thus the larger square was related to the smaller one in the ratio $\sqrt{2}$. If Street used such a technique at the Fortune it is likely that he had found it already in the old fabric of the Theatre and had therefore used it in the Globe, the Fortune's general model. The *ad quadratum* scheme is readily adaptable for use with the sort of concentric circles that formed the basis of the Globe's plan, as is shown by the traditional diagram of it that Sebastiano Serlio printed in the introductory book of his *Architettura* (illustration 37). Our best chance of checking the groundplan of both the Globes is provided by Hollar's drawing, for Norden's view of the first Globe's roof is too slight to be of value in matters of such precision. The second Globe occupied the first's foundations and therefore shared its plan, and a careful measurement of Hollar's sketch shows that it too was proportioned *ad quadratum*, the diameter of the yard equalling that of the whole house divided by $\sqrt{2}$ (allowing, as before, for measurement through post centres rather than wall surfaces).

The proportions of the Globe's floor plan were evidently established by traditional means, but it remains to discover the overall size. Here, in this altogether crucial matter in which the very character of the house is so obviously at stake, no contemporary document has any direct evidence to offer. We know that the Fortune was 80 feet square, and that the yard in which the Boar's Head playhouse was established was an irregular shape some 54 feet 6 inches deep and as

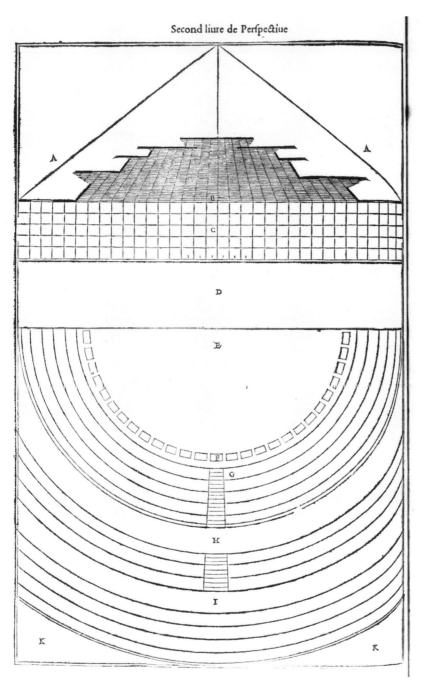

*37: Serlio's* ad quadratum *scheme, from* The First Booke of Architecture, *1611.*

much as 121 feet 5 inches wide along its greatest dimension. Beyond that, history is silent, or curiously misleading. We may assume, for example, that most of the playhouses were of a similar height. De Witt shows the Swan with three storeys of galleries; three storeys are shown in the engraving of the Theatre and are described in the contracts for the Hope and the Fortune. Indeed this last document gives measurements which, because the vertical requirements of headroom are fairly standard, may be taken as typical. First there is a brick foundation rising 'one foote of assize att the leiste above the grounde'; then come the three storeys of 12 feet, 11 feet and 9 feet respectively, so that the total is 33 feet to the plates. If we were to take Norden's view of the Swan literally, and apply the 33-foot measure to its height as he shows it (in three storeys, incidentally), its overall width would scale at about 40 feet. An even narrower proportion would result from a literal interpretation of the engraving of the Theatre, and of course Visscher, ever faithful to his model, gives the same proportions as Norden's Swan, though transferring them to the Globe. It is obvious that these depictions are not to be taken at face value, if only because they allow insufficient room for both stage and audience. We know that the stage at the Fortune was 43 feet across, while that at the Red Lion in 1567 was 40 feet by 30 feet; and we are told by de Witt that 3000 people could crowd into the Swan, a figure independently repeated some twenty-five years later by the Spanish ambassador when talking about capacity houses at the Globe itself. No 40-foot polygon could contain all this.

As before, we turn with gratitude to Hollar's fine depiction of the second Globe. Built on the same foundation as the first, this playhouse must also be the same size overall. With some confidence, then, we measure the height of the outer wall as given in the drawing, taking its base to be roughly at the foot of the bushes which obscure it to the left. The whole width of the frame is easily measured, and we divide the larger figure by the smaller and multiply the result by the assumed 33-foot height of the frame. The conclusion is staggering: according to this admittedly rudimentary calculation the diameter of the Globe is almost 110 feet, far larger than any reconstructor has proposed hitherto. Yet the figure is based on what is beyond dispute the most reliable of the documentary evidence that has come down to us. Unless there is something wrong with our method we shall in all conscience have to accept it.

And of course there *is* something wrong with our method. Hollar's study is accurate enough, but its precision is of a specialized sort that must be understood before it can be coaxed into yielding its secrets. Many of Hollar's drawings of London are wide panoramic views which range such landmarks as church towers and spires along a broad horizon like marks on a calibrated scale. There is something almost mechanical about these drawings which invite comparison with the surveyed facts of the topography as registered on a modern map, and it has recently been demonstrated that some of the panoramic views do indeed represent an accurate plane section across the sightlines to the landmarks from a known point of view.[23] It seems that Hollar must have made use of a drawing frame or 'topographical glass' to give so accurate a survey of the scene. Such devices were in fact much used by topographical artists, and are described in contemporary artists' handbooks (illustration 38). Hollar's study of west Southwark may be plotted against the modern map in this way, (illustration 44) and the resulting diagram analysed trigonometrically to yield the diameter not only of the Globe but of the Hope as well. The linear perspective conditions produced by the careful use of an optical device would tend to overstate the diameter of 'round' buildings at some distance from the centre of the view, a distortion which can be exactly calculated and taken into account. The diameter of the Globe has been calculated at 102.35 feet and that of the Hope at 99.99 feet, both plus or minus 2 per cent. While still larger than has hitherto been generally supposed, these figures are not so great as that yielded by the simpler – but probably naive – method of comparing the width of the Globe to its height. The Hope, moreover, is shown to be approximately the same width as the Globe, and it appears that there may have been a standard Elizabethan public theatre frame design, some 100 feet or so across and probably developed *ad quadratum*. The Hope, after all, was specified in its contract to be the same size as the Swan; and if these were the same size as the second Globe they were also the same as the first, on whose foundations it stood. And this in

[113]

turn, constructed from the timbers of the Theatre, presumably repeated its ground plan and size.

The first Globe, then, like many other Elizabethan theatres, was 100 feet or so across. Like the Fortune it was designed *ad quadratum*, so that its yard was 70 feet in diameter, post-centre-to-post-centre. Its shape, governed by the fact that it was a timber structure, was a polygon, but of many sides rather than few. Street's geometric cast of mind suggests that the number would be one that might be yielded by the manipulation of surveyors' lines on the ground: a multiple, say, of six and/or four.

There is some analogous evidence that may be of help here. A plan of the Swan appears in an estate map of Paris Garden Manor (1627), showing the theatre as a series of concentric circles apparently drawn with compasses.[24] The outer two are divided radially into fifteen sections, suggesting perhaps that the building had fifteen bays. The division is not very regular, and may be merely a rough freehand indication of an unidentified number of divisions. Very much earlier, at Calais in 1520, Henry VIII's workmen constructed a vast wooden theatre, polygonal in plan and consisting of three storeys of galleries placed about a central arena. Although it was covered by a great double canvas roof supported like a tent by a central mast, it may well have been an ancestor of the Elizabethan theatres. Contemporary witnesses are agreed that its polygonal frame had sixteen sides.[25] And finally, much closer to home, the Swan as depicted by de Witt appears to have had twenty-four sides. The drawing shows what seems to be one half of the frame, and to the left of the tiring house we may count four bays, with three to the right. The tiring house itself may be judged to obscure five more bays for a total of twelve, or twenty-four in the whole structure. Of all these figures, the last comes closest to satisfying our requirements: it is large enough to have suggested a round plan to de Witt, it is closer in date to the building of the Globe than the Calais house, and it is a satisfactory multiple of four and six. In short it is a figure altogether in harmony with Peter Street's methods of design and such scanty evidence as we have on the matter.

No contemporary view shows anything of the interior of the first Globe, but the cooperative scholarship of recent years has gone some

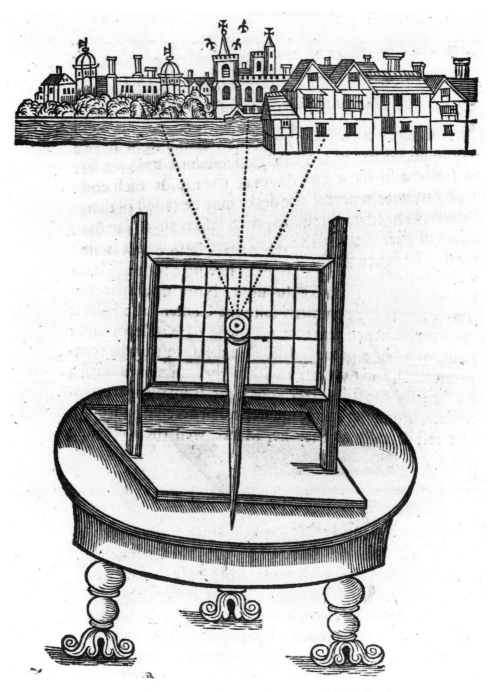

*38: A 'topographical glass' or drawing frame as used by Hollar from
the tower of Southwark Cathedral, from John Bate,* The Mysteryes
of Nature, and Art *1634.*

*39: Hollar's survey of west Southwark, plotted on a modern Ordnance Survey map.*

way towards providing an understanding of its structure. Contemporary observers, and especially those who disliked theatres, agreed that they were 'gorgeous' and 'sumptuous'. John Ronayne has likened them to those wondrous cabinets of the sixteenth century whose plain outsides belie interiors which sparkle with colour and intricate carving when the doors are opened.[26] The inner richness was remarked by de Witt at the Swan, whose columns he reported to be painted to resemble marble. Peter Street was specifically required by his contract not to complete the finishing of the Fortune, the extra work being placed elsewhere–presumably with a member of the Painter-Stainers' Company–at a cost of £80. When the Fortune burned in 1621 a contemporary reported that it had been 'the fayrest play-house in this towne',[27] an epithet which, we recall, had already been applied–and by the same observer, as it happens–to the second Globe. Playhouses were, we may conclude, typically 'fair', even if only one could be the fairest of them all.

De Witt shows an elevated stage from which rise two giant columns supporting a tiled roof and curious superstructure. The drawing is not

[116]

without its problems of interpretation, as we have already had cause to notice, but this lower roof must be related to the 'shadowe or cover over the . . . Stadge' which was included also in the Fortune contract, and there too required to be covered with tile. We know that there was a 'heavens' at the Rose in 1595, and although there is no evidence that such a device was a usual fixture in the earliest London theatres, it is likely that the Globe would have had one in 1599.[28] Its style of decoration can only be guessed at from a few possibly descriptive allusions in the plays. We hear of a 'marble' heaven in both *Othello* and *Timon of Athens*. In the latter it is called 'the marbled mansion all above' (IV iii 194); and so it is too in *Cymbeline*, a play that was certainly performed at the Globe, even though it was written with the Blackfriars also in mind.[29] We know that the Swan was painted to look like marble, although it was actually made out of wood, and de Witt found the imitation so convincing that it stood up under the closest scrutiny. At the Fortune the 'Stadge' was plastered with lath, lime and hair–presumably this clause referred to the stage *frons* and the ceiling above.[30] A plaster ceiling painted to imitate stone therefore seems likely to have been provided at the Globe.

It will possibly have been decorated with some sort of cosmic or zodiacal theme, but this is unlikely to have been a single-field painting. Hamlet evidently alludes to the Globe's stage roof when he describes the 'canopy' of the sky as 'fretted with golden fire'.[31] 'Frets' in contemporary plasterwork were moulded ribs which divided the whole area of a ceiling into panels or compartments. The intersections of the ribs were marked by bosses which were often gilded, and could well have been fashioned to represent stars. It happens that during the period of the Globe's construction a particularly active school of plasterers flourished in London and Middlesex, and there survive several examples of their work. An enormous ceiling at Canonbury is even dated, on a central panel, 1599–the very year of the Globe. From these examples we shall be able to derive an idea of the design that most probably enlivened the Globe's stage cover with moulded panels of the planets and the signs of the zodiac.[32]

The stage in the de Witt sketch of the Swan is fronted with two ambiguous things which might be supporting piers or dark gaps where hangings have been left a little apart. Neither interpretation of these cursory lines is very convincing, and one can only react to them with a raised eyebrow. We know that the Fortune's stage was 'paled in belowe with good stronge and sufficyent newe oken bourdes', perhaps to prevent the groundlings in the yard from penetrating its understage mysteries. Here the contract's evidence is much clearer than de Witt's, and should be followed in our reconstruction. The Swan's stage is elevated by a little under one-ninth of its width, or about 4 feet 8 inches if the platform is taken to be 43 feet across like that at the Fortune. It is rectangular in plan, and evidently reaches exactly halfway across the yard, just as the Fortune's was required to do by the contract. It is a reasonable though not a certain conclusion that the Globe's stage was also elevated, rectangular and brought to the diameter of the frame. The stage at the Red Lion was 5 feet high – it is the only case where the height of an Elizabethan public playhouse stage is precisely known – and because this figure broadly agrees with de Witt it will be adopted in our scheme on Bankside.

With the superstructure over the 'heavens' we come to one of the more problematic of the features shown in the de Witt sketch. Previous interpretations of the drawing have described it as a 'hut' built across the trusses of the stage roof, and used for housing descent machinery and other devices.[33] But since the publication in 1983 of the documents describing the Red Lion, with its great stage tower erected within the playhouse yard, some interpreters have begun to recognize what should perhaps have been obvious all along: that de Witt shows a stage tower rising within the yard of the Swan. Its lower storey, clearly drawn well forward of the main frame galleries, is marked *mimorum aedes* (the actors' house, or tiring house); the middle floor is devoted to boxes for spectators (the so-called 'lords' rooms'); and the top – again deliberately drawn forward of the main frame – is a lofty station for the flag and trumpet that announce the afternoon's performance across the neighbouring rooftops and over the river towards St Paul's. There is no 'hut': no Elizabethan account book or contract mentions such a thing, and it would in any case be structurally awkward.

[118]

The Swan and the Red Lion both possessed these great stage towers, though only the Swan added a stage roof to the front, supported by two giant columns. The picture of the Theatre in the engraving of London seen from the north shows what appears to be such a tower rising within the playhouse yard. But the most reliable of all the depictions of a contemporary theatre is Hollar's sketch of the second Globe, which is there recorded as being equipped with a very different kind of structure over the stage. Instead of the tower rising independently within the arena, a huge twin-gabled roof covers one side of the yard, stretching all the way across it and firmly tied in to the timber work of the main frame. This roof rises to a grand height, certainly, and it has a decorative lantern at the top, but its very presence precludes the sort of stage tower found so much earlier at the Red Lion and the Theatre. Presumably the Globe's integral roof was installed during the rebuilding of 1614, but it is essential to discover whether its design had been anticipated at the first Globe, or whether the players had merely re-erected the stage tower from the Theatre when they moved its timbers to Bankside.

Lacking better evidence, we turn to the etchings and engravings of seventeenth-century London. Most were—as we know—prepared far away in Antwerp or Amsterdam by artists who were never in England (or, in the case of Jodocus Hondius, who had left its shores before the Globe was built), and used one another's prints as their main—and usually their sole—sources. Only Norden's *Civitas Londini*, prepared and published in London in 1600, can be much relied on, but this gives us the two contradictory views of the newly-built Globe. In the small map the round frame has a stage tower rising within it; in the panorama is a most interesting stage roof which presents a gable end towards the centre of the yard. In this it anticipates the form of the second Globe's roof as depicted by the meticulous Hollar, though in a much simpler, less adorned, single-ridged design. According to Norden, then, the first Globe *may* have had a turret like that at the Theatre; or again it *may* have had an integral stage roof tied in to the main frame, a less-developed form of the second Globe's great cover.

Which of the two forms are we to adopt in our reconstruction? (For we may now confidently set aside the 'hut' formulation based on

[119]

Visscher which influenced our earlier designs.) Stage tower or integral roof? In 1986 we convened a large seminar at Pentagram Design in London, and thrashed the matter out. In the end the decision was made to follow Norden's picture in the panorama, partly because it led to a fine and practical design and partly because it seems unlikely that Norden could mistakenly have set down a roof that so clearly anticipates the design of the second Globe. In preparing new drawings for the project Theo Crosby found that it was necessary to raise Norden's integral roof above the ridge line of the main frame in a way that again anticipates the form recorded by Hollar.

Next to the stage stands the 'tiring house', the place from which the actors emerged to play their roles, and in which they made themselves ready. The sketch of the Swan shows it rising within the yard, the lower storey of the stage tower. Possibly the bottom part of the Red Lion's tower had also been given over to this use. At the Boar's Head playhouse, fitted up in a Whitechapel innyard in 1599, the same year as the Globe, the tiring house was constructed beneath a gallery that ran across the back of the stage; it did not form any part of a tower.[34] If the Globe itself had the integral type of stage roof recorded by Norden it too had no stage tower, and it is not clear whether its tiring house was built standing out in the yard as at the Swan and Boar's Head, or was simply fitted up in the part of the main frame that was contiguous with the stage. The contract for the Fortune theatre required Peter Street to set up both the stage and the tiring house 'within the frame', a phrase that presumably means 'within the yard formed by the frame'. Since the Fortune was generally based on the Globe it may very well be that the Globe's tiring house was also set up 'within the frame' in this way, that is, standing out in the yard. Few previous attempts at reconstructing any of the playhouses have followed the weight of the evidence in this matter, because a tiring house in the yard seems to be a serious inconvenience.[35] It obstructs sightlines and diminishes the depth of the stage considerably, while leaving the bays of the main frame behind it with no apparent function. At present, therefore, our designs retain the idea of a tiring room fitted up within the timber-work of the main frame, its front forming a chord across five of the bays. But the matter clearly deserves re-examination.

The main features of the tiring house are given, *faute de mieux*, by de Witt, save that the Swan's two stage entrances have been increased to three, as seems to be required by the internal evidence of the Globe playtexts. The scheme shown by de Witt reminds one of the Tudor Hall screens with their doorways and minstrels' galleries, and in developing a detailed design for this part of the Globe, which we assume to have been the 'fairest' and most delicately painted of all, we have been guided particularly by a drawing made by Robert Smythson for a screen at Worksop Manor (*c.* 1585). The doors, we may suppose, opened inwards towards the tiring house, so that curtains or hangings of 'arras' could be hung along the lower storey of the front, and the central entrance will have been made large enough – presumably double-hung, like the Swan's doorways – for the 'discoveries' occasionally required by the plays.

I am acutely aware that in this chapter I have been able to survey only part of the tangled forest of difficulties encountered by anyone who sets out to recover the design of the Globe. Fortunately there have been many investigators, patient, dogged folk who, loving the tumbling vitality of the Elizabethan drama, also admire the distant beauty of its theatres.

Many have contributed to the Bankside project, through their published work and more personally in committees and correspondence. Most have been governed by the ideal of reconstructing the Globe *as it was*, though nearly all have known from the start that even if we could be sure of every detail of the building as it stood in 1599, certain compromises would be inevitable. The fire which consumed the first Globe must not be permitted to raven down the reconstruction too, and we shall have to instal a sprinkler system. The dangerous thatch will not do, so we have opted, like the King's Men when given their second chance, to cover the house with tiles. The open yard would permit smoke to escape in a disaster, and the heavy oak construction of the building is not in itself an undue fire hazard. Nevertheless modern regulations require more escapes than the 'two narrow doors' through which the audience emerged on St Peter's Day 1613, and the two staircase turrets must be made larger than those shown in Hollar's drawing to accommodate exits made to modern standards. There will have to be some electrical wiring for the necessary exit signs, and possibly to give the best equivalent we can achieve of the light that must have been provided at the original Globe late on a winter afternoon by cressets and rush candles. The seating cannot in all conscience be provided to scant Elizabethan standards, which no modern audience would endure. Good evidence from the Court and university theatres of the seventeenth century shows that the normal allotment of seating space was 18 inches both sideways and fore-and-aft, and in the latter dimension at least we shall have to exceed the original by far. Such plans as we have of the earliest theatres make little or no allowance for access passages and steps for the audience, but these too will have to be provided on Bankside, designed to modern specifications.

Fortunately the main parts of the structure will remain unaffected by this regiment of modern imperatives. The great stage will rise among a crowd of groundlings, whose standing places in the yard will, I trust, be as cheap as those in the arena at an Albert Hall prom; the frame will rise above them, oak-built and painted like marble, fitted with degrees on which the majority of the audience will sit; while high above, oversailing like a gaudy cloud and supported by its tall Corinthian columns, the 'heavens' will shade the stage. Here at last, in the wood and plaster ring close by the Thames, the strutting player will once more be able

> To hear the wooden dialogue and sound
> 'Twixt his stretched footing and the scaffoldage.[36]

Nor does every modern requirement come with the unanswerable authority of a fire regulation. In his earlier project schemes Theo Crosby was not much concerned with the historical orientation of the first Globe, and so placed it as to bring the backstage area close to Skin Market Place, the alley that leads along the southern boundary of the site. His aim was to allow the best possible access for a loading dock, and this left the theatre facing about 7.5 degrees east of north. But the recent discovery that the Globe actually faced about 48 degrees east of north – a discovery based on a technical analysis of Hollar's sketch – brought some hitherto unsuspected considerations with it. [37] For one thing, 48 degrees is close to the azimuth, or compass-point, of the midsummer sunrise at Southwark's latitude. The original Globe seems to have faced in much the same direction as Stonehenge, and while there is no evidence for any particular significance in this fact it might well be unwise to ignore it. Of more immediate importance was the recognition that the Globe's stage must usually have been shaded by its cover and the surrounding frame if it was located in the southwest quarter of the theatre. This matter seemed worth testing, and a large model of the Globe was accordingly placed on a movable table that could be tilted and turned in the beam of a profile spotlight to imitate the exact penetration of sunlight into the playhouse for particular times of the day and year. [38] Some of the results for the 48-degrees orientation are given in illustration 5; they show that in the afternoon performance hours (GMT) the stage was invariably and totally shaded, even at midsummer when the sunlight penetration of the frame was at its greatest. Some, though not very many, of the audience would occasionally have the sun in their eyes, but they would always be looking at a shaded stage. Clearly this disposition is the reverse of what our modern prejudices would lead us to expect – we are accustomed to dark auditoria and well-lit stages – and the effect is so complete and unambiguous that it clearly reflects a deliberate intent on the part of Peter Street and the Lord Chamberlain's Men. There was some debate about whether we could afford to follow the original builders on the present site, with the consequent severe restriction of the backstage access, now that the stage itself will be turned away from Skin Market Place. In the end Theo Crosby struggled to bring the theatre round to its home bearing, and the advisory committee decided, as it had done so far on every occasion when a choice was possible, to opt for authenticity. I like to think that generations of scholars would agree with them.

*40abc: Views by Hollar of the Blackfriars theatre.*
*Top: Seen from the prospect room at Durham House.*
*Bottom: Details from Hollar's etchings of London, showing it before and after the Great Fire of 1666.*

# CHAPTER 4

# THE INIGO JONES DESIGNS

## *by John Orrell*

During his working lifetime Shakespeare probably had an important say in the design of three playhouses used by the Lord Chamberlain's (later the King's) Men. In 1596, while the company was still at the Theatre in Shoreditch, James Burbage purchased part of the old Dominican priory that lay something over a mile away, to the south of St Paul's, between the cathedral and the river. There he constructed an enclosed theatre for performances by candlelight. When they were prevented from transferring to this new house, the players built the Globe; and whether or not Shakespeare had a direct personal hand in the design of either theatre it is certain that they were both developed with the presentation of his plays in mind. Later, when the Globe burned down, the players rebuilt it 'far fairer' than before; but in the meantime they had established themselves also at the Blackfriars. Any complete study of the canon of Shakespeare's plays must take account of this influential stage, for it too was a significant part of the physical plant at the playwright's disposal.

The Blackfriars was an enclosed playhouse, very different from the half-open Theatre or Globe. It was located in the old 'upper frater' of the priory buildings, in a large upper chamber which had once held parliaments and even the legatine trial of Catherine of Aragon. Burbage's deed of 1596 gives some details of the property from which it is possible to deduce, with the aid of later leases, that the space available for the theatre was 46 feet by 66 feet, internal measure. A drawing by Hollar showing London as seen from the prospect room at Durham House upriver gives a tenuous sketch of the building, and it appears again in the same artist's etched views of London before and after the Fire of 1666, although by then the theatre itself had been replaced by tenements.[1] The structure had thick stone walls – Richard Hosley has estimated them at 5 feet thick – and if it resembled other fourteenth-century monastic buildings of a similar type they will have risen some 32 feet above the floor level or, allowing for a vaulted undercroft and the declivity of the site, as much as 59 feet above grade at the southern end.[2] The ridge of the roof will have brought this latter dimension to something over 85 feet, a dizzy height and one that fully justifies Rosencrantz's allusion to the boys' company that occupied the playhouse there before 1608 as a nest of squeaking baby hawks:

> . . . there is, sir, an eyrie of children, little eyases, that cry out on the top of question and are most tyrannically clapped for't. These are now the fashion, and so berattle the common stages – so they call them – that many wearing rapiers are afraid of goose-quills, and dare scarce come thither.
>
> (*Hamlet* II. ii. 339–44)

The auditorium was probably reached by a great winding stair mentioned in the deed as abutting the northern end of the upper frater.[3] It was constructed in a 'great Hall or Rome' whose integrity was restored by the removal of old partitions, and across one end (presumably the south, opposite the stairs) was a stage running east to west. There were galleries and somewhere up above, possibly among the rafters, there were further rooms.

From here on, unfortunately, almost everything we know about the physical structure of the Blackfriars is ambiguous or speculative. Some prefatory verses by Leonard Digges printed in the 1640 edition of Shakespeare's *Poems* give a dim glimpse of the interior:

> . . . let but *Beatrice*
> And *Benedicke* be seene, loe in a trice
> The Cockpit Galleries, Boxes, all are full . . .
>
> (sig. *4ᵃ)

We may suppose that the galleries surrounded the pit, and that some part of them may have been dedicated to boxes. But in 1632 an altercation took place at the Blackfriars when a dandy stood on the stage and obscured the view of spectators sitting in a box. One of these stretched out his hand and 'putt him a little by', provoking an instant and dangerous sword thrust in reply.[4] The box must therefore have been within an arm's length of the stage and much on a level with it; if it was to one side it will doubtless have been answered by another opposite, and the stage itself must therefore have been at least two box-depths narrower than the chamber. The shape of the auditorium is unknown, though various academic reconstructions have favoured a rectangular plan with three levels of galleries following the right angles of the room.[5] But Ben Jonson, in the Induction to his Blackfriars play *The Magnetic Lady* (1632), brings a snobbish spectator on stage to complain to one of the theatre employees about 'the *Faeces*, or grounds of your people, that sit in the oblique caves and wedges of your house, your sinfull sixe-penny Mechanicks . . .'[6] 'Caves and wedges' are odd words to find in a description of an auditorium, but they correspond in a rather pedantic way to the *cavea* and *cunei* into which the round of an ancient Roman theatre was divided. This suggests that the Blackfriars galleries were segmental or U-shaped in plan, perhaps in imitation of the theatre scheme published by the Italian architect Sebastiano Serlio, whose work profoundly influenced Elizabethan designers. Such a plan would account for Sir William Davenant's description of the Blackfriars audience:

> Conceive now too, how much, how oft each Eare
> Hath surfeited in this our Hemispheare,
> With various, pure, eternal Wit . . .[7]

'This our Hemispheare', we may suppose, was constructed by James Burbage at a time when the Blackfriars was seen as a possible successor to the Theatre. If the galleries were thus rounded in plan the dead corners at the northern end may have been used for access stairs to the upper levels. To the south the stage with its flanking boxes had at least two entrance doors, for several playscripts assuredly connected with the house require them, and probably a third, which was needed for *Eastward Ho*:

*Enter Maister Touch-stone, and Quick-silver at several* [i.e. separate] *dores . . . At the middle dore, Enter Golding discuering a Gold-smiths shoppe, and walking short turns before it.*

(*Eastward Ho*, sig. A2ᵃ)

[127]

Evidently the middle door could be used for small scenic 'discoveries', and was probably larger than the other two. There was some sort of acting space above, and music was sometimes stationed there behind a curtain. A single trap door was sparingly used, and there was a descent machine allowing vertical drops on to the stage. For the rest we know nothing specific, though the intelligent use of analogical evidence from other theatres – notably the Fortune contract – has enabled reconstructors such as Irwin Smith and Richard Hosley to arrive at a remarkably complete if necessarily speculative view of the playhouse.

From the moment in 1609–10 when they mounted their first play there, the King's Men at the Blackfriars transformed the London theatre world. Hitherto the boy players had offered a rather special-ized and perhaps slightly erotic sort of entertainment, powerful enough in its heyday to threaten the economic wellbeing of the adult players. But now the best adult troupe in London took over the enclosed theatre and performed before smaller audiences in the intimacy of candlelight. From the boys they may have inherited a specialized local audience consisting partly of the Inns of Court lawyers and their students, together with the well-heeled dandies of the town who came to flaunt their plumes seated on hired stools on the narrow stage. They inherited too the boys' special bent for music, retaining the habit of instrumental playing between the acts of the drama. All this became part of Shakespeare's artistic property at about the time when he turned to the composition of *The Tempest* and *Pericles*. The Globe was of course still fully in his mind as he wrote these plays, but he would have been curiously indifferent to have ignored the new opportunities offered by the Blackfriars, and we notice how musical and masque-like *The Tempest* is, and what fun is had with effete courtiers in *The Winter's Tale*.

The Blackfriars, then, represents a second side to Shakespeare's artistic milieu, one that might so easily – but for the strenuous objections of the local community – have entered the complex equa-tion of his creative talent at a time when he was thinking of *Romeo and Juliet*. In proposing to reconstruct the Globe on Bankside the International Shakespeare Globe Centre quite rightly sees as its central task the building of the great amphitheatre itself; but in recent years it has also undertaken to include in the project some representation of the Blackfriars side of Shakespeare's working world. The ideal would be a reconstruction of the upper frater itself, complete with its vaulted undercroft and thick masonry walls. But the speculative nature of the reconstruction outlined above makes such an undertaking a risky affair. Almost every part of the structure would be based on analogical rather than direct evidence, and of course the whole would be extremely expensive because it would be necessary to recreate the medieval shell within which the Elizabethan playhouse was erected.

It happens, however, that there exists a set of drawings by Inigo Jones for a theatre almost exactly like the Blackfriars, if a little smaller and presumably a little chaster (or more Jonesian) in design. They belong in the great collection of Jones's drawings which is held in a couple of weighty albums in the library at Worcester College, Oxford. For nearly 300 years, they lay with the rest of the drawings in their press, catalogued by the architectural historian J. A. Gotch as having some connection with the Barber-Surgeons' Hall in Munkwell Street, until in 1969 Professor Don Rowan of the University of New Brunswick spotted their interest for the theatre historian and published them for the first time.[8] Still, Dr Rowan offered no opinion about the actual identity of the theatre they showed, a matter to which we shall turn soon. Once published, the drawings began to find echoes of recognition on every side. For here (illustration 41) was a building which integrated in a satisfactorily complete design most of the elements we know to have been present at the Blackfriars.

The Inigo Jones theatre is an enclosed house with a raised stage built across one end. There are boxes flanking the stage to either side, placed exactly so that a seated person could reach out and push aside some swaggering fool standing on the stage itself, just as happened at the Blackfriars. Here, finely articulated in Jones's earlier manner, is a *frons scenae* with the three entrance doors of the Blackfriars, the central one wide enough to effect the 'discovery' of Golding's shop in *Eastward Ho*. At the upper level there is a framed and pedimented aedicule for the music, or for use as a small upper stage and obviously capable of being characterized – as the upper level often was – as a 'window'. In the section the stage itself is omitted, but it shows up in the plan, where it is equipped with a balustered rail along its front. At its foot is a semicircular pit, surely the 'Cockpit' of Leonard Digges's account of the Blackfriars, and it is equipped with seating (again shown only in the plan) in the manner of the private theatres. There are only two storeys of galleries, where the Blackfriars perhaps had three, but their plan is unmistakably rounded, like Davenant's 'Hemispheare'.[9] There is no sign of the stage trap or descent machinery of the Blackfriars, but there is room for both and indeed more than generous headroom among the roof trusses for the latter.

Jones gives the scale for his drawings, showing that while the theatre is somewhat smaller than the Blackfriars it is not so by a very wide margin. Its external width is 40 feet and it is 55 feet long, as against the (presumably internal) dimensions of 46 feet by 66 feet at the Blackfriars. Both would have been intimate houses, but there is a real possibility that Jones's would actually have been cramped. The two smaller stage doors are only 5 feet 6 inches tall in the clear, and hardly large enough for impressive entries. Any trapwork under the stage would have been undertaken, so to speak, in a headroom of hardly more than three feet, unless the floor were excavated in a fashion not shown in the section. But the seating, though desperately small by modern standards, is no more compressed than in other contemporary theatre designs, allowing 18 inches fore-and-aft, with special seating ledges at the front of each degree. Allowing 18 inches of lateral bench space for each spectator, the capacity of the house is about 700, far less than the Globe of course, but perfectly agreeable with our notions of the smaller audiences of the private theatres.

In short it appears that the drawings at Worcester College, whatever their precise identity, show something remarkably like the Blackfriars. So like the Blackfriars, indeed, that an early decision was made at the International Shakespeare Globe Centre to attempt to include the theatre in the Bankside project as adequately representing the type of enclosed house towards which the Lord Chamberlain's Men were drawn in 1596 and at which the King's Men eventually thrived after 1609. The reasons for the decision are, I think, sufficiently obvious. To begin with there is the sheer difficulty of reconstructing the

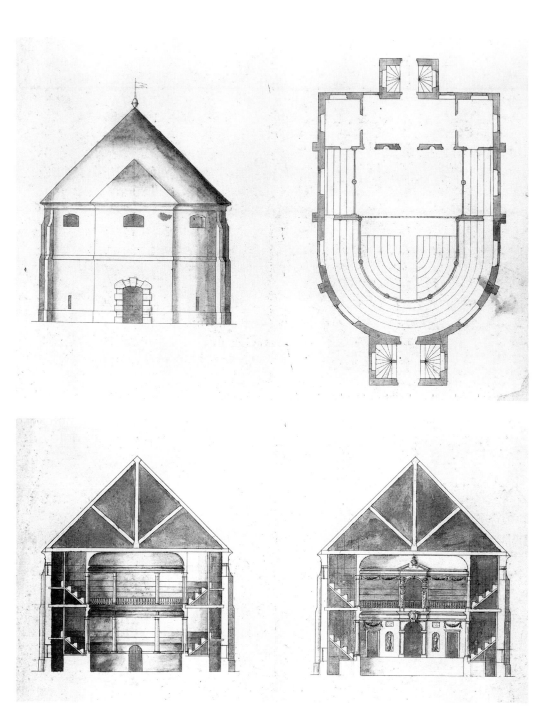

*41: The Inigo Jones drawings for a hall playhouse, probably made in 1616.*

Blackfriars playhouse even on paper, when so little of the evidence about it is directly relevant to its physical structure. Of course brilliant attempts have been made to rise above these difficulties, but the results are certainly at least as speculative as the reconstruction of the first Globe. Then again there is the fact – not without its influence on the ambience of the house – that the Blackfriars was an upper-storey room, perched like an aerie high above the Thames.

To recreate such a structure would be expensive, and much of the expense would have little direct theatrical benefit. On the other hand Jones's drawings provide us with the kind of concrete certainty that all Elizabethan theatre studies unfortunately lack. Here we have a merciful gift, and one it would be monstrous to refuse. Each part of the building is precisely delineated, in both plan and section, interior and exterior. We have its scale, the exact relation between stage and auditorium, a plan of the tiring rooms and an elevation of the stage gallery. We know the pitch of the roof and the height of the string course and water table. Here for once the English theatre historian can leave his guesswork and address two sheets of paper generously spilling over with unimpeachable facts.

Some of the facts help to explain others which hitherto have been puzzling. An example is the balustraded gallery over the stage, in which are shown, to either side of the central aedicule, rows of stepped degrees evidently intended for part of the audience. Except for the small central area, where no degrees are marked, there is room for seating all around the stage at this upper level, even in the part that is presumably behind the players' backs as they address the main round of the auditorium. Now, it is a curious fact that of the four contemporary pictures we have of sixteenth- and seventeenth-century London theatre interiors, three show people seated in just this strange location. Indeed the Swan drawing depicts no audience at all except for the row of spectators in the stage gallery, and in a tiny vignette on the title page of William Alabaster's *Roxana* (1632) some players are shown on a small railed stage with audience members both in the pit and in the tiring house gallery. As in the Swan drawing the performers address the pit or yard rather than the gallery behind them, and exactly the same is true of a late depiction of an indoor stage which appears in the frontispiece to Kirkman's *The Wits* (1662). Here in the Restoration we have certainly moved on from the Jacobean theatre in some respects—there is, for instance, a row of footlights where the *Roxana* stage has a rail—but still the fundamental arrangement is the same, with audience members both fore and aft of the actors. The fourth picture, another tiny vignette, from the title page of Nathaniel Richards's *Messallina* (1640), shows no spectators and no actors, but the railed stage resembles that of the *Roxana* print. The stage gallery here has shrunk to a curtained music room, the space to either side of which is represented as a blank masonry wall, probably simulated rather than real. [10]

The identity of the theatres shown in these seventeenth-century prints is unknown, but in scale they appear to show something akin to the Inigo Jones playhouse. There are, of course, many differences. A minor one is the presence of hangings behind the players and underneath the stage gallery or music room. Jones makes no provision for these, but it is not difficult to see how they could be fitted to his *frons scenae*, attached to brackets underneath the balustrade. A far more important difference is the shape of the stage, which is shown in the *Roxana* and *Messallina* vignettes to taper towards the front, thus implying—though without actually showing—that audience members could take up positions to either side of its thrust. The *Wits* frontispiece includes spectators sitting in this position, even though the stage itself in this case is a rectangle. Not one of the pictures shows the sort of stage-side box from which one might lean to ease aside a swaggering nincompoop standing on the stage itself, as happened at the Blackfriars. But Jones's theatre does supply this very feature, thus making it all the more convincing as an analogue of the Blackfriars.

Indeed the most exciting quality in Jones's drawings is their secure sense of how an Elizabethan or Jacobean private theatre must have worked, their grasp of the quite fundamental facts about the relation between actors and audience. Here is an intimate enclosed house, obviously intended for candles rather than natural light. Yet it is not altogether tiny. One need only pace out its dimensions to get the feel of its scale; when I try it in my own small suburban garden I am very soon out on the pavement and even into the street when I try to fit in the stair turrets. Forty feet by 55 feet at any rate is far bigger than most people's houses, and the candles would have much work to do late on a December afternoon. Once on stage, the players—I locate them here by the flowerbed—would find the mass of spectators in front of them, across the stage rail (and taking up the space to the fence at the bottom of the garden). These would constitute Davenant's 'Hemispheare', but there would be others ranked in two storeys of boxes to either side of the stage and a further group in the tiring house gallery. The playhouse was therefore a somewhat modified theatre in the round, with audience on all sides, and the very furthest of them only some 32 feet away from an actor standing at stage centre.

Once we have apprehended something of the scale of Jones's theatre we can try to imagine a few of its working details, beginning with the stage. The section of this end of the house does not show the stage itself in place—evidently Jones thought of it as a removable structure independent of the frame of the building—but the sills of the entrance door indicate that it was elevated to a height of 4 feet. The plan shows that it was equipped with a rail, somewhat in the manner of the *Roxana* and *Messallina* vignettes, and in a drawing by John Webb of the Cockpit-in-Court theatre at Whitehall we find a scaled cross-section of such a feature, showing it to be some 1 foot 3 inches high and substantially made of fat-bulbed balusters which both Jones's plan and Renaissance precedent required to be closely spaced on centres six inches apart.[11] Of course even the flimsiest rail would constitute a major barrier between the player and his public, but the solid affair implied here would quite seriously impede the sightlines from the pit, though leaving the gallery spectators with a clear enough view. The stage would, in fact, seem to be fenced in by the stage-box rails to either side and the stage rail to the front. We should be unwise, therefore, to think of the Jones theatre—or, for that matter, the Blackfriars—as simply arranging the closest possible contact between actor and audience. In matters of scale and physical disposition it does offer such intimacy; but what it gives with one hand it takes away with the other, setting up barriers that serve to distance the stage from the auditorium. Anyone having the least acquaintance with the dynamics of Shakespeare's acting texts will recognize this tension between the 'pull' of empathy and the 'push' of alienation, their exploitation from moment to moment of the diverse possibilities of the physical stage. The tug-of-war with the audience is everywhere in the canon of the works, but one famous example will serve to illustrate them all. The assassination of Caesar on the Ides of March is something any audience will anticipate with little enough prompting, but Shakespeare heightens the expectation by every available means: narrative, prophetic, even symbolic when Casca indicates the direction of the Capitol in II. i. 110–11 by pointing his sword at it. Tension heightens when the troubled Portia sends a message after Brutus, and when Caesar turns the soothsayer aside. It mounts still further when Popilius Lena hints to Brutus and Cassius that he has heard of their enterprise, then passes beyond them to talk – disarmingly, as it turns out – to Caesar. As our anticipation rises we are forced at this moment to contemplate Caesar in dumbshow mediated through the dialogue of the others. Then the conspirators make their move, encircling their victim, kneeling at his feet: he has become the centre, first of the group of petitioners and next of the surrounding audience, whose fiercely aroused anticipation makes them participants in the violent act that follows. 'I am constant as the northern star'; then the knives and '*Et tu Brute*'. The deed is done, and in the emotional release that follows there is Cassius chasing the receding tide of our feelings with his imaginative evocation of the event as the source of future dramas:

> How many ages hence
> Shall this our lofty scene be acted over,
> In states unborn and accents yet unknown!
> (*Julius Caesar* III. i. 112–14)

– as, for example, the state of England and the accents of W. Shakespeare. The conceit is challenging, thought-provoking, and above all self-referring. The intensely lived-through event of a moment before has become the food for thought, and we in the audience, already emotionally confused by the aftermath of the blood-letting, find ourselves elbowed into a reflective mood. If this scene were to be played in the Inigo Jones theatre the encircling intimacy of the house would surely aid the play's tautened anticipation; seated in the encircling galleries or in a box beside the stage itself, we should join the close-pressed throng of spectators as assistants at the near ritual of the slaying, what Brutus attempts to define as a 'sacrifice'. And then, with that tension released in the flurry of commands and comments after the killing, we should reel back, encouraged by Cassius, to contemplate the play as 'sport', as something to be looked at and possibly to be pondered. During the assassination itself who would notice a thing as unimportant as a stage rail, no matter how substantial it was, or how much in the way? It would simply vanish, as invisible as the rest of the theatre. But afterwards, when Cassius calls the event a 'lofty scene' and Brutus talks of Caesar bleeding 'in sport' the rail would re-establish itself as a boundary between the fictive and the real.

The origins of the stage rail are obscure, but it must have been there for the actors rather than the audience. It has been suggested that it would prevent rowdy fellows in the pit from climbing on to the stage, but in Jones's theatre it would only have given such people a useful hand grip on the way up. For the actor it doubtless provided somewhere useful to sit, where he might have the best contact with the entire audience (at 1 foot 3 inches it was just the right height for such a perch); it might also prevent him on occasion from dropping unannounced into the pit; but most important of all, it represented the magical, penetrable border between the play and its audience.

Let us pass, then, from the stage to the auditorium. The distinction is at best ambiguous in this theatre, because the latter surrounds the former. At the upper level, indeed, there is seating on all four sides in one continuous sweep broken only by the pedimented music room. These 'degrees' are high (just over 40 degrees) and anyone seated in them would have a positive sense of towering above the players. Access to them is by way of a passage along the rear wall, where the going, though dizzily steep, would be eased by a number of vertical posts rising through the rearmost degree. (Only two of these posts are shown in the section of auditorium, but they should probably continue at intervals all around the curved part of the house.) The passage is lit by a series of small segmentally-headed windows whose light, though visible from many parts of the house, is high up, well away from the stage, and unlikely to cause a distracting glare. At the lower level the galleries can surround the stage on only three of its sides, the fourth being devoted to the stage entries, but the effect is still one of encirclement. Here the four rows of degrees are reached, as they are above, by way of an access passage at the rear, but this has no windows, presumably because their light would be uncomfortably close to the sightlines of those sitting opposite. At the lowest level is the pit, whose degrees, though shown in the plan, are omitted from the section, perhaps because they were removable. They have six risers, but the total height available for them before the foot of the lower gallery rail is only 3 feet, so their rake must have been much shallower than that of the gallery degrees. Standing at the centre of the house a spectator might look about and see the gradual rise of the pit degrees step up more sharply from the point where they meet the blank rail of the lower gallery. Here functional posts with Doric capitals rise to support the gallery above, where a balustered rail makes a clear decorative effect. At the upper level there are more posts superimposed on those below, and given capitals of Corinthian proportions, but without the acanthus carving. These upper posts have no structural function, the ceiling above them being attached to the roof trusses whose load passes directly to the brick piers of the shell. Perhaps Jones intended to evoke in them the colonnade of an ancient Roman *porticus*.

At the Blackfriars, we recall, Ben Jonson thought of the audience in terms of 'caves and wedges', *cavea* and *cunei*, yet unlike the Roman theatre the stage was flanked with spectators' boxes. Inigo Jones's theatre also compromises the Roman scheme in this way, encircling the stage with places for the spectators. And yet there is in the design a curious feature which, like the stage rail but with even greater emphasis, breaks across the pattern of the theatre-in-the-round. In the plan Jones marks a heavy brick wall between the rounded auditorium and the stage boxes. Its presence is further acknowledged by the fact that the degrees in these boxes are not quite continuous with those in the galleries, but are set back one step to either side. To effect the junction between the ill-matched sets of degrees, the wall between them, marked in the sections as rising only to their bases, will almost certainly have been brought up the full height to the roof trusses, thus effectively closing off the house side of the theatre from the stage side. Of course a good part of the audience would have been accommodated in the four boxes and the upper gallery of the stage side, but the barrier in the plane of the stage front will have been very marked, its presence registered yet again by the different widths of the coved ceilings over the two halves of the house. Only by running an architrave or compartment element between the two ceilings could Jones satisfactorily join them, and such a device, coved on both sides, would link with the vertical structures we have posited to form something very like what later ages would call a proscenium arch, or at least a permanent structure into which a regular seventeenth-century stage 'frontispiece' could be inserted. Arches for scenic purposes had been used occasionally in Tudor Court stages[12] and the scenic frontispiece became a hallmark of Jones's masque designs, appearing also in the theatres he designed specifically for plays at Court.[13] Nothing about the drawings for the enclosed theatre gives an indication that it was originally planned as a scenic house, but if it was constructed to Jones's extant plans it would have been easily convertible to scenic uses, though to be sure with a much reduced audience capacity.

There is no certain evidence that the Blackfriars was ever used for the production of plays with scenery, and it seems unlikely that it shared the adaptability of the house shown in Jones's drawings. The scenic possibilities of his design almost certainly reflect his own preoccupations, which would not have been shared by James Burbage when he converted the upper frater in 1596. The Blackfriars is unlikely to have been equipped with anything like a proscenium arch. Nevertheless at least one of the private theatres that stood in London during the first third of the seventeenth century was capable by 1658–69 of housing scenes, for in that year William Davenant staged his production of *The Siege of Rhodes* at the Cockpit in Drury Lane, with scenes by John Webb. The subsequent history of the playhouse shows that it could accommodate some elaborate French 'machine' plays with spectacular changes of scenery and vivid descents and cloudwork. There is some sign too that it was equipped with scenes by Jones as early as 1639. Nevertheless it certainly began life as a regular private house of the Blackfriars type, and in its earlier years it was famous as the regular competitor of the King's Men's theatre.

Thus far I have considered the Jones drawings simply as an adequate representation of the theatre form which Burbage embraced when he shaped the Blackfriars in the expectation that it would be used by the Lord Chamberlain's Men when their lease at the Theatre in Shoreditch ran out. It is obvious that the Jones drawings are not actually of the Blackfriars, for the shell of the building is nothing like the upper frater of a Dominican priory. But the drawings are painstakingly executed to presentation standard, the kind of thing that might be offered to a patron as a record of his commission. They are not theoretical pieces, labelled for textual commentary, nor are they mere whimsy. Their high quality is a sound indication that they were made for a serious project, whether or not it was ever actually built. It is not surprising, then, that attempts have been made to identify the theatre they show. First, Professor Glynne Wickham nominated the Salisbury Court playhouse, built in Dorset Garden close to the Thames in 1629. Very little is known about the physical structure of this theatre, but it was set on a plot only 42 feet wide and in later years a dancing room was erected over the upper part of it, measuring 40 feet square.[14] Jones's theatre is 40 feet wide externally, and therefore fits these Salisbury Court dimensions very well. Unfortunately the evidence ends there, and is hardly sufficient to establish an identity, especially when set against the fact, reported by Professor Rowan when he first published the drawings, that their watermark is much earlier, with a latest date of 1616.[15] Of course Jones could have used old stock as late as 1629, but one would feel happier with an earlier identification. John Harris, the Keeper of Drawings at the RIBA, then set on record his judgement that the style of draftsmanship dated the drawings to 'between *c.* 1616 and *c.* 1618'.[16] Not everyone agrees with Harris's dates—Gordon Higgott, for example, would place them much later—but they do coincide both with the evidence of the watermark and the fact that the other major private theatre of seventeenth-century London was erected in 1616. This was the

Plate IV: The Inigo Jones theatre as it might have been in 1616. See note on p. 182.

Cockpit in Drury Lane, converted by Christopher Beeston from a regular commercial cockpit, and dedicated at its opening for use by the Queen Anne's Men, who wore the livery and enjoyed the patronage of the Queen herself, whose prime London residence was only a few hundred yards away in Denmark House (otherwise known as Somerset House). The first to suggest the identification of the drawings with the Drury Lane theatre in print was Iain Mackintosh, and soon it found widespread if not universal acceptance.

The history of the Cockpit is longer and in its way more varied than that of the Blackfriars. It began in 1609 as an ordinary arena for cockfights, built by John Best, cockmaster to Prince Henry. Such buildings were quite small, generally round in plan and with a conical roof. A typical size would be 40 feet in diameter, with a pit at the centre capable of taking a 12-foot table for the birds to fight on, surrounded by three or four rings of degrees rising to an ambulatory or standing place set high against the perimeter wall. In 1616 Christopher Beeston took over the lease of the cockpit and set about converting the structure to theatrical uses. This act caused some comment from the neighbours, a little of which got into print, with the result that we know that the work did not involve complete demolition and rebuilding so much as extensive structural alterations. Beeston was soon in trouble with the authorities for proceeding with new construction work 'att and adjoyninge to the Cocke-pitt'. Specifically he and his bricklayer were charged with building on a new foundation, contrary to the oft-renewed royal proclamation against such enterprises, whose object was to prevent the overcrowding of the city by restricting development. Nevertheless, though summoned to appear before the magistrates, Beeston proceeded and his theatre duly opened.

Faced with the need to expand a circular cockpit Beeston could either demolish and begin anew, or he could add to one side of the circle and so create a U-shaped plan like that in Jones's drawings. We know from the neighbours' comments that he eschewed the former alternative, and the proclamation against new building would combine with practical necessity to urge the latter upon him. The terms used by the court recorder—'att and adjoyninge to the Cocke-pitt' – precisely confirm that this was Beeston's course. The most recent version of the proclamation allowed the extension of existing buildings provided that the new part was no larger than one-third of the old, and although Jones's drawings imply a greater expansion than that it is not difficult to see that they might have been argued past the authorities. If Beeston did indeed have Jones's name to conjure with there would be little enough need for argument, for the Royal Surveyor was deeply involved in current work for Queen Anne, including stage work at Denmark House, and his word would carry persuasive weight, both with the Middlesex justices and with the Privy Council to whom they might appeal. It is, I think, significant that when the Benchers of the nearby Lincoln's Inn sought to prevent what they called 'the covertinge of the Cocke Pytte in the Feildes into a playe house', they took their complaint not to either of these major authorities, but direct to Queen's Council, Anne's own advisory body.[17] As lawyers, they knew what strings to pull.

Not that it helped. The playhouse was built, and at Shrovetide the following year it was assaulted by gangs of rowdy apprentices. Damaged during this affray it nevertheless soon reopened, and was sometimes thereafter called the Phoenix, though the original and simple title proved the longer lasting, remaining its exclusive name in the Commonwealth and Restoration years. Beeston's control over the house was firm, and after the death of Queen Anne various troupes of players came and went while he stayed on to manage the house and cream off the profits. The Cockpit became established as the chief competitor of the Blackfriars, and a methodical survey of the plays performed in it shows that it must have had at this time precisely those features that are shown in the Jones drawings: a raised stage with three entrances, the central one large enough for discoveries, and a small upper acting level, but probably no trap or descent machine.[18]

In 1637 Christopher Beeston established at the Cockpit something of a novelty: a company of boy players for whom he had arranged a notably direct royal patronage. On 21 February a warrant was issued from the Lord Chamberlain's office 'to sweare Mr Christopher Bieston his Majesties servant in ye place of Gouuernor of the new Company of the Kinges & Queenes boyes'.[19] Not only were the boys doubly crowned by this recognition, but Beeston himself became a specially appointed officer of the royal Court. Though he did not survive to enjoy his status very long – he died in 1639, his post passing directly to his son William – it was during this regime of close royal patronage through the Lord Chamberlain's office that Inigo Jones drew a scene design for an unknown play, jotting across the top the endorsement, 'for ye cokpitt for my lord Chamberlain 1639' (illustration 48). Some have thought that this drawing must have been intended for the Cockpit-in-Court at Whitehall, but that theatre was so constructed as to make the introduction of complex scenery almost impossible. By contrast the other London Cockpit of the time – if the Drury Lane theatre is indeed the house shown in the Jones drawings we have been discussing – could readily accommodate a set of scenes like these. The frontispiece is contained approximately within the proportions of a square, just as high as it is wide, and would fit perfectly the opening of the stage towards the auditorium in Jones's theatre. We can measure the opening from the two sections by taking the height above the stage to the top of the *frons* entablature, and the width of the auditorium between the gallery posts. In his sketch Jones shows the frontispiece erected in the same plane as a stage rail, so that in the theatre drawings it would have to be mounted at stage front. The system of scenery shown in the sketch places a group of three flat wings, each representing a tent, to either side, spaced so that they narrow towards the back, where a pair of shutters has presumably been withdrawn to reveal what Jones usefully describes as a 'citti of rileve': a structure of profile flats set up before a backcloth and representing a townscape in superimposed layers.

In order to mount a play equipped with such scenery at the Jones theatre it would be necessary to sacrifice all the audience seating on the stage side of the frontispiece, possibly as much as half the capacity of the whole if the dead areas at the back of the galleries close to the stage are discounted. Nevertheless the remaining seats would hold about 300 people, enough perhaps for a special Court performance laid on by the Lord Chamberlain.[20]

While the Lord Chamberlain's scene is of a proportion that can readily be fitted into the Jones theatre, we do not know its precise

42: *A sketch for a scene in a play at the Cockpit, Drury Lane, made in 1639 by Inigo Jones.*

scale and therefore cannot be certain of the exactness of the fit. It is true that the size of the stage rail shown in the sketch gives some indication that the scenery was small enough to have fitted the Jones theatre, whose relatively shallow stage could well have accommodated the three-wing depth required by the design; but this type of evidence lacks precision. What we need is an exactly-scaled scene design that we know to have been used at the Cockpit and that can also be shown to fit the Jones theatre like a glove. Such evidence, though still circumstantial, would be persuasive. Fortunately it happens that almost two decades after Jones dashed off the Lord Chamberlain sketch, when Charles I had lost the country and his head and when Jones himself was dead, William Davenant transferred a production of his so-called 'opera' *The Siege of Rhodes* onto the Cockpit's stage. Its scenes were designed by John Webb, whose measured drawings for them still survive. Over the years there had been changes at the Drury Lane theatre, but its major fabric still stood, and it can be demonstrated that Webb's designs fit it precisely.

*The Siege of Rhodes* originally opened at Davenant's home in Rutland House, and in a preface to the published edition of the play, dated August 1656, he apologizes for the small scale of the enterprise:

It has been often wisht that our scenes . . . had not been confin'd to eleven foot in height, and about fifteen in depth, including the places of passage reserv'd for the musick.

Webb's frontispiece for the work (illustration 43) is ruled up 11 feet high by 22 feet 4 inches wide, the whole being mounted on a stage 3 feet high. In the British Library is a drawing by Webb showing the plan and section of a raked stage similarly fitted with scenery 11 feet tall and 22 feet 4 inches wide, but only 2 feet 6 inches high at the front and 18 feet deep. It is deeper therefore than the 15-foot Rutland House stage and must show the other house to which *The Siege of Rhodes* transferred, the Cockpit in Drury Lane. Here in 1649 the Parliamentary troops had broken up the stage and evidently the old *frons scenae*, but two years later William Beeston had refitted the house at a cost of £200.[21] In Jones's original section of the stage end of his theatre the space available for a stage structure, measured between the

*43: John Webb's frontispiece for* The Siege of Rhodes, *1656.*

brick piers he shows to either side of it, is exactly 22 feet 4 inches, the width of Webb's stage and frontispiece. Moreover the frontispiece shown mounted on the British Library section of the raked stage reaches a height of 13 feet 6 inches, precisely matching the first-storey entablature in the theatre; and the entablature itself is 2 feet tall, just the same as that in Webb's frontispiece. In short, the British Library stage is a perfect match for Jones's theatre, which we may now identify with some confidence as the Cockpit in Drury Lane.

It has been necessary to review the evidence of scenery at the Cockpit in order to establish the identity of Jones's drawings. But the review serves a second and more important purpose when it reminds us that the history of the English theatre in the seventeenth century saw the quite rapid replacement of the older rhetorical sort of playhouse by a new scenic theatre, and the adaptation of many old plays (including Shakespeare's) for the new conditions. If we build the Jones Cockpit playhouse to these precise and original designs we shall possess a structure which comes as close as we dare hope to the staging conditions established at the Blackfriars by James Burbage in 1596 and inherited by Shakespeare in 1609. But we shall also have a house which is capable of being adapted to accommodate scenery of the type shown in the Lord Chamberlain sketch and of the exact dimensions given in Webb's drawings. We shall not, of course, want to imitate the Parliamentary troops and destroy the *frons scenae*, and any scenes in the theatre will have to be contained within the 15-foot depth of the original design, but by a very simple expedient we can remove the level stage and replace it with a raked one capable of taking Webb's scenes or others of a similar size. In building Jones's Cockpit, therefore, we shall have not only the equivalent of the Blackfriars, but the capacity to explore the revolution in staging techniques which was so completely effected in the years after the Restoration.

# CHAPTER FIVE

# THE COMPLETE COMPLEX

## 1. APPROACHING THE BUILDING

It was never going to be possible just to rebuild the two playhouses without fitting them into a larger complex, a frame for the stories they tell. Precisely as the description of the original designs of the playhouses in this book had to be put into the context of the original companies which used them, their original performing conditions and their original audiences, so the rebuilt playhouses have to be presented as the main exhibits in a display which will make it easy for the visitor to see them in the right kind of historical perspective. Essentially the rebuilt playhouses are the central feature of a re-created piece of London's history

The display of the two playhouses and the many little stories which belong with them will give the background for the Globe's original design, and the story of how that design evolved through the playhouses built in the years from 1567 to 1599 in London. It will also tell the story of how the Globe's success led to its partnership with the Blackfriars hall, and how Shakespeare's company ran its repertoire of plays through the great years from 1599 to 1642. It will show where the Inigo Jones playhouse belongs in the later story of the Globe, and the impact of the hall playhouses on production by Shakespeare's company. It will also show what effect the Court productions of masques and plays staged with scenery might have had on Jacobean and Caroline performing traditions.

In the complex as it is to be built the Globe itself will stand on a piazza raised well above ground level, so that it is fully visible above the river wall to anyone looking across the river from the north, along the range from Blackfriars Bridge to Southwark Bridge. Positioned opposite the great dome of St Paul's, it will in its very different way match it as a great landmark of Thames-side history. Under the piazza will be two spacious areas, artificially lit, which will provide 12,000 square feet of floorspace for the exhibits which tell the story of the Globe. Visitors will be able to begin with the exhibits on these lower levels, including scale models of several of the early playhouses, before climbing the stairs to see the Globe itself. The rebuilt playhouse, and its companion the Inigo Jones playhouse, will be the climax and finale to the static displays which make up the 'museum' element in the visit.

The Globe, its gallery roof standing 36 feet above the piazza, will dominate views of the complex from across the river. Its polygonal shape, white walls and black roofing will make it stand out from the buildings surrounding it. These related buildings, including the Inigo Jones theatre, the foyer and lobby to the exhibition complex, the restaurant and cafeteria, and the shops which flank the Globe piazza, will show a variety of styles of façade, some matching the seventeenth-century baroque of the Wren House which the complex will abut others with their own distinct styles. The roofline of the complex as a whole will not only include the Globe's circle of the gallery ridges and the 'huts' or stage superstructure looming over the galleries, but the distinctively baroque gable front of the Inigo Jones building. Behind it will emerge a baroque square tower and lantern for the lift tower, and on the opposite flank the squared roof of the apartment block which links to the Wren House on the western flank of the complex. The Globe itself, largely separated on its piazza from the other buildings and linked to them from beneath, will give the complex its essential identity. The related buildings will, except on the river front, surround and pay homage to it, each in its distinctive fashion.

The story which will be told by a visit to the Globe begins with the different forms of transport available for getting to the Bankside. Inevitably these have changed since 1600, along with everything else. Coaches and taxis can trace their way to Emerson Street and Park Street by any of the routes London has accumulated in the centuries since the Globe brought its first customers there. But there are versions of the older routes, too. The new customer who chooses to retrace the original paths will be able to take a modern version of either of the forms of transport that were available to the Elizabethans. The more affluent can go, like the Elizabethan gentry, by boat, although the kinds of boat and the piers at which they board the boats have changed. They can take a ferry from upriver or downriver, from Westminster or Greenwich. The new landing for the Globe will be at the pier which in the 1940s and 1950s satisfied the Bankside Power Station's voracious appetite for coal. The wherries which were sixteenth-century London's nearest equivalent to taxicabs are long gone, as is the old London Bridge which provided the other early form of transport to the Bankside's varieties of pleasure, travel on foot. Today the simplest access on foot is from Blackfriars across Blackfriars Bridge, and turning left along the waterfront till the Globe comes into view. Alternatively, and more attractively, the site can be reached from further east by crossing Southwark Bridge. This latter route, from the central section of the old City of London, not far from the site of the old London Bridge of Shakespeare's time, has the advantage of taking the visitor close to the site of the original Globe.

As you cross Southwark Bridge from the north bank of the Thames, in the heart of the City, you first see a row of elegant eighteenth-century houses, Anchor Terrace, on the south bank to your left, inclining less than enthusiastically and rather ominously over Southwark Bridge approach. Under it, and under the approaches of the bridge, lie the remains of the original Globe. As you come to it, though, you should turn right and descend the steps to Park Street – or better still, you may already have descended to Bankside itself and the river front, the direct path to the Globe, which is no more than 100 yards to the west of the bridge. If you take the longer route along Park Street you will miss the river with its splendid view of St Paul's and the smaller brown and white outline of Wren's elegant St Benet's Church on Paul's Wharf. But you will pass beside some of the other marks of Southwark's famous theatrical past. Rose Alley is named after Philip Henslowe's Rose playhouse, the first playhouse to be built on the Bankside, in 1587. Its original location was at the end of this alley. (The Rose Alley where the Poet Laureate John Dryden was beaten up in 1679 by a gang of thugs hired by a rival was not this one, but an alley of the same name in Covent Garden.) On the western corner of Rose Alley is the Bear Gardens Museum, prototype for the Globe complex and now providing offices and rehearsal space.

The Bear Gardens lane itself is named after the kind of building which first attracted Philip Henslowe and his enterprises to South-wark – the bear-baiting amphitheatres, one of which stood on the site of the Museum. The Hope, which was built to double as a bear-baiting house and a playhouse in 1614, and which is visible along with the Globe in Hollar's 'Long View', was located here. One of the minor ironies of the modern Globe site is that the man who owned the land in the days when Shakespeare and his fellow-players were building the original Globe playhouse a few yards away was their great rival, Philip Henslowe.

A right-hand turn at the next lane, Emerson Street, leads straight back to the river and to the Globe complex. Made into a pedestrian walkway, tiled and cobbled, it leads past the main entrance of the exhibition centre to the river with its superb view of St Paul's and the City. If visitors should choose to walk a little further on, as far as the river frontage itself, they will find that Emerson Street also delivers up a first close view of the Globe. The riverside walkway which runs (or strolls) the mile or so along the Thames from the Festival Hall and National Theatre at Waterloo comes past here on its way to the former church of St Mary Overies, now Southwark Cathedral, where Shakespeare's brother is buried, on the other side of Southwark Bridge. This is the route which the visitor crossing by Blackfriars Bridge will join. From the river front the full scale of the rebuilt Globe can be measured with the eye. That middle-distance view will be worth taking, because once inside the complex the Globe will be on view much more intimately and in close-up.

Like most functional spaces, the entrance foyer to the exhibition offers many things. It gives access to the cloakrooms, and for educational parties the orientation room. It gives direct access to the Inigo Jones playhouse, the theatre most likely to be in regular use through the evenings. It also gives access to the cafeteria and restaurant, services likely to be demanded by some before, some after, and no doubt some during the tour of the whole exhibition. The tour ends where it begins, in this foyer, so all the main services, including the lift to the different floors, have their access here.

In the foyer visitors can obtain a cassette commentary or a 'docent' guide to accompany them on the tour. Two kinds of tour will be on offer. The basic one provides a direct introduction to the story of the Globe and the related subjects on display. The longer one takes the more curious or more leisurely visitor into some of the byways which branch off the main story. The tour is not by any means unidirectional, a single straight path along a line of exhibits. It was thought to be of the utmost importance to make it an exploratory exhibition, catering for a wide range of possible interests, and offering the chance to satisfy a variety of different forms of curiosity. Essentially the story to be told step by step through the exhibition will be the creation of the Globe, but it will have many sidesteps, and three major paths.

## 2. THE EXHIBITION

The essential story on display at the International Shakespeare Globe Centre's complex concerns a building, Shakespeare's workplace. Around that central thread two others are entwined, the setting in London, especially Southwark, and Shakespeare's own life as a player. The story gives a detailed account of the architectural history from which the design of the workplace evolved, an outline of the operating conditions of the players, including Shakespeare, for whom it was designed, and some displays to show what it was like in operation.

The forms which we use to tell this story vary as the details of the story vary. For the material features of the buildings we can use models, both of complete playhouses and of sections or details from the different kinds of structure used for playhouses up to 1642. There are plans, diagrams and models for the student who wants precise details of the playhouses contemporary with the Globe. There are films using modelscopes to show the insides of some of the models.

There are stills presenting large-size reproductions of the sixteenth- and seventeenth-century illustrations that survive as the main evidence for the shape of the playhouses. There are videos illustrating particular features, both of the 'hard' elements in the buildings and the animated activities which were the purpose for which they were built. Finally there is a cinema for large-screen viewing of Shakespeare in performance.

The main display covers most of the basement floor of the complex, beneath the piazza on which the Globe stands. The visitor begins by descending to the exhibition level, and then follows a carefully guided but thoroughly winding course, full of what Henry IV, in a very different context, called bypaths and indirect crooked ways, through the various displays. Some of the bypaths are likely to prove irresistible, others may be too tangential or stray too far from the intentions or interests of the visitor. As a 'free' tour, without any direct guidance or parties or packaged programmes, it offers a maze to be threaded in individual ways towards the final destination, the reconstructed Globe and Inigo Jones theatres. The range of individual interest is likely to be so various that it would be contrary to the spirit of the whole concept to push visitors through on a predetermined schedule. It is experimental and educational in the sense that it should provide the means for different people to satisfy quite different kinds of curiosity without the frustration either of being overwhelmed with too much information or cut off from further exploration. The main floor of exhibition space will be a kind of labyrinth, without a minotaur and with free access to the exit from any point. Each visitor will be a Theseus with his own ball of string, unwinding the Globe story from section to section of the exhibition. The string of the entwined stories will sooner or later lead the visitor to the exit, the stairs which go up to the piazza and the Globe itself.

The main string of the exhibition tour begins with an account of some of the chief characters in the story. These will include the players, notably Shakespeare, Richard Burbage, Will Kempe, and Edward Alleyn. There will also be the playhouse builders, including James Burbage, Philip Henslowe and Peter Street. Not least, there will be the London playgoers of the time. Their lives will be shown, set in their time and their town, the London of 1600. Its sights, sounds and possibly even its smells (though the conspicuous play-house smells, tobacco and garlic, are still quite familiar enough these days) will be backed up with a graphic account of London's rapid growth through the period of Shakespeare's lifetime, mapping its geographical spread, the shifts in population density, and the distribution of wealthy districts and poorer suburbs. There will be an account of its trade and traffic routes, especially the river traffic so basic to life and work in Southwark. Such local items in Southwark as the St George's brickfields, which most likely supplied some of the building materials for the Globe, will be described. A note about the governmental structures of the City, and the more lenient govern-ment of the northern and southern suburbs ruled over by the magistrates of Surrey and Middlesex will lead on to an account of the constraints that geography and local government laid on playhouse-building and the entertainments industry of the time. Then the entertainments themselves will be shown, a display focusing closely on Southwark itself. The bear- and bull-baiting, the brothels, and the succession of Bankside playhouses will feature in detail.

The London audiences require a section to themselves, lavishly illustrated from contemporary prints and paintings. The class struc-ture and the way it manifested itself in the playhouses will be shown, covering the range of social types from the 'understanding men' in the yard, apprentices, house servants and artisans, to the citizens in the twopenny rooms and the gentry in the lords' rooms. These divisions in society and in the playhouse auditorium will be illustrated by pictures of the social types and by diagrams of where they chose to fit themselves in the two kinds of auditorium: the amphitheatres and the halls. A special section will describe the women playgoers. This will include the range of different social types, and also the special constraints that women suffered under. There were many of these. There was not only illiteracy, but the requirement that a respectable woman should be accompanied wherever she went, whether she was a Court lady followed by her page or footman, or a citizen's wife with her husband's apprentice, or fishwives and applewives who came to the playhouse in parties or in family groups. In playhouses an unaccompanied woman was all too readily assumed to be a whore. The social range from whores to the supreme lady, Queen Elizabeth herself, will be on display here. The social audience section will conclude with a description of the Court, its location, its premises and the halls where plays were staged, its social characteristics and above all its chief characters, Queen Elizabeth and her Stuart successors.

The story then shifts to the players. A brief account of the rising of acting companies in England in the sixteenth century will begin with the travelling players. It will be possible to study an enlarged facsimile of the 1572 Act of Parliament designed to restrain idle vagabonds, with its special exemption for the companies of players which had official approval. The first licence issuing a royal patent to a company of players, which legitimized James Burbage's company in 1574, can also be studied here. An account of Richard Tarlton, the most famous clown of the time, and his company the Queen's Men, set up to create a royal monopoly in 1583, will lead up to the story of the companies run by Henslowe at the Rose in the early 1590s and the establishment of the Chamberlain's Men, with Shakespeare as a sharer, in May 1594. Documents from Court records making payments to sharers in the company, including Shakespeare, and facsimiles of the title pages of plays which list the actors who first performed in them will accompany other evidence, chiefly from the Henslowe papers, showing how the playing companies operated. Facsimiles of the 'parts' written out for each player to learn his lines from, of the 'plot' which hung in the tiring house to show the storyline of each play, playbills, title pages of some of the most famous plays and the ways they advertised the story, will all be on show in the appropriate tiring-house setting. Costumes, including wigs (black skullcaps of tightly-curled wool for 'blackamoors' like Othello, long blond tresses for ladies like Desdemona), riding boots, cloaks, doublets, half-armour and some of the more portable trappings such as rapiers and 'dags' pistols will accompany this section of the exhibition.

The story next moves on to the evolution of playhouse design. In this section the concern is largely with the precursors of the Globe, the open amphitheatres which developed from the innyards and baiting arenas with their surrounding 'scaffolds' of galleries. Complete models and sections of models, together with a graphic display of the step-by-step development of the playhouse structures, will form the main feature of this section. The tower over the stage which was a feature of the Red Lion, the earliest known amphitheatre playhouse, will be seen altering its shape as it evolved into the gabled 'shadow' or heavens of the first Globe and the double gable of the second Globe. Some account, necessarily conjectural, will be given of the different forms of access for the audience. These seem to have developed from the early progression where everyone entered the yard first, and then if they chose paid more to go on into the galleries, into the later system used at the Globe, where the entrances at the base of the stair towers gave an immediate choice of access either to the yard or up the stairs into the galleries. This section will also look into the way in which the design of the stage and the tiring-house front or *frons scenae* developed. Hall screens and their gradual elaboration, including an increase from one or two entry doors to three, will be illustrated with pictorial examples. The development of hall screen design apparently in parallel with the evolution of tiring-house fronts, and the increase in the number of entry doors in hall screens matching the increasing numbers of doors on the stages of the various amphitheatres, will be graphically displayed from surviving examples.

And then we come to Shakespeare. His career from Stratford to London will be sketched in, noting his early residence in Southwark through the 1590s, the record of the burial of his brother (also a player) in Southwark Cathedral, his purchase of property in the Blackfriars in 1613, and his retirement to Stratford. A reminder of the busy life of the player, tied in London to the company, or going wherever the company was travelling when plague closed the London playhouses, stands against Shakespeare's consistent engagement with affairs at home in Stratford. His business in London, the two plays a year that he supplied to the company, the parts he is said to have performed in his own plays (the ghost in *Hamlet* and Adam in *As You Like It*), the kingly parts at which he was said to excel, the few material facts we have about Shakespeare's working life, all belong here.

[157]

The story moves on through the broad sweep of events in the later 1590s (briefly outlined in Chapter Two) when the company was losing its playhouse and desperately scratching around to raise the funds to build themselves a workplace. The plays they let the bookseller Andrew Wise publish in 1597 and 1598 to raise money, the lawsuit they brought against the playwright Thomas Dekker in 1598 to recover a debt (probably a loan for writing a play, even though he was supposed to be contracted to Henslowe), and the legal tangles the Burbages got into with Richard Allen, the owner of the Theatre's site – all these small features of the Globe story are material details which can be put into the context of the company's struggle to get a permanent playhouse.

The Blackfriars playhouse, which might have made it unnecessary for the Globe ever to be built, and which eventually came to outshine it in popularity at least among London's gentry, looms on both sides of the Globe story, before and after. Here, then, stands the Blackfriars playhouse in model form, and with it the exhibition's story about playgoing and performing in the hall types of playhouse. And alongside the Blackfriars stands the story of the Inigo Jones playhouse, the full-sized reconstruction of which waits for a visit after the Globe.

There is another story to be told here, about the third kind of playing venue for Shakespeare's company. The hall playhouses offered performances to rival the amphitheatres for all but a few of those busy years from 1576 to 1642. Until 1609 they only had weekly performances by boys who, like the adult companies, played in the afternoons. But the Shakespeare company was also summoned at regular intervals to the royal Court. Performances at Court were special occasions, by royal command and paid for from the royal purse. They took place in the evenings, by candlelight. Sometimes the performances might simply be set in a banqueting hall, as they would when the company was summoned to perform for a nobleman and his friends. Sometimes one of the Court's special playing places might be used. The palace at Whitehall, for instance, had an old cockpit, built in the time of Henry VIII, which was sometimes used by the professional acting companies. In 1629 Inigo Jones redesigned it on Palladian principles, with a curved tiring-house front and five entry doors, decorating it lavishly. A plan survives for this playhouse too, together with the accounts for its decoration.

A model and facsimiles from the accounts relating to the decoration of the royal Cockpit at Court provide one of the most spectacular sidetracks of the whole exhibition. In Stuart times plays at Court were only one of the various forms of entertainment offered during the festive seasons. Court masques, by far the most lavish and spectacular shows of all, became a special art in Shakespeare's time. Ben Jonson wrote the scripts for many of them under King James, and Inigo Jones designed brilliantly ingenious staging devices. Descriptions and drawings for many of these have survived. The players took the speaking parts in these spectacles of music, dancing, oratory and visual scenic effects. Both plays and masques staged at Court were part of a Shakespearean player's work. The displays of what they were involved in when they came to Court form a necessary and colourful part of this third kind of theatre venue.

Back in the main story line of the Globe and Shakespeare's company's struggle to find a playhouse to replace their lost Blackfriars, comes their rivalry with the Philip Henslowe playhouse and its companies. The implications of Shakespeare's company's decision to move to Southwark alongside the Rose and the Swan, and Henslowe's prompt decision to move in the opposite direction into the northern suburbs which the Chamberlain's company had abandoned, can be shown graphically. The precise layout, history and character of the Bankside parish in Southwark will be mapped out here, along with the peculiar story of Francis Langley's Swan and the order made by the Privy Council in 1597 to have it pulled down.

And of course there is the account of the building of the Globe itself. By far the most substantial part of the whole exhibition, it will set out in careful detail the full story of how the Globe playhouse first arose on Bankside in 1599, and how the original was recreated for the modern Bankside, as it has been described here in Chapter Three. The original evidence from Hondius, de Witt, Hollar and the others will be accompanied by detailed architectural drawings, models and videos of the whole design as it has been rebuilt. The story of the Theatre and the use of its timbers for the Globe's framework, the art of the sixteenth-century builder and his *ad quadratum* measuring techniques, carpenters' markings as seen in contemporary wooden structures, photographs of wooden-frame structures from the time, and a survey of different roofing methods, both thatch and tile, will be amply illustrated in a display using static pictures, video displays and computer graphics. A survey of Elizabethan techniques of wall decoration and colouring will lead to conjectural reconstructions of possible forms of decoration for the Globe. Similarly, conjectures about the hall screen models for the tiring-house front will be shown in model and graphic form. Finally a step-by-step account of the way the design was calculated, and an examination part by part, with visual close-ups of the design, will be included as the culminating feature of this section.

The story of the Globe is far from finished there, of course. Before the visitor has access to the great reconstruction itself, there must be two more extensive sections to strengthen the sense of time and place which are so necessary for a sound appreciation of the structure. The first, a lengthy and well-illustrated display of properties and scenes, will tell what is known about performance at the original Globe. It will try to convey some impression of the actor's intimate closeness to his audience. It will outline the schedule of the original performances, including a graphic depiction of the effects of sunlight and shadow through the course of an afternoon's performance. It will detail the range of admission prices, and show the gatherers and their tricks for secreting the coins which they were supposed to drop into their collecting bags. It will present the stage properties, including the thrones and the four-poster beds which were 'thrust out' for their appropriate scenes, and the drums, trumpets and banners which signalled armies on stage. It will show brief scenes exemplifying ways in which the plays might have been staged at their first performances. There will be a section of computer keyboards and screens offering two-dimensional line depictions of the Globe stage on which the visitor can manipulate stage figures and properties to try out different versions of the staging of particular scenes and the movements of characters around the stage platform.

A vital accessory and an extension of this climactic part of the exhibition, the Globe at work, is the large-screen video display. The audio-visual resources of the ISGC will make available a huge variety of screened excerpts from the plays. Visitors will be able to call up favourite versions of particular scenes or make comparisons of different actors playing the same scenes. Both small-screen videos for the single visitor and large-screen showings of Shakespeare on film for groups make an important contribution to the sense of Shakespeare in performance which is the proper prelude to the experience of the Globe itself.

Finally, before the visitor climbs the stairs to the piazza level to try out his or her stretched footing on the Globe's scaffoldage, and to test the acoustics and the lighting effects in the open-air auditorium, there is a little more history. The Globe did not last forever. The fire of 1613 which destroyed the first Globe and the construction of its successor are the features of this last section. Along with those stories goes the history of the King's Men and their outstandingly successful record of playing unbroken right up to the closure of 1642. The main features of the Blackfriars playhouse loom here along with the whole history of the hall playhouses. Their exclusion from this story of Shakespeare's Globe would distort history by removing the alternative that James Burbage designed in 1596 before the Globe was ever conceived. Its great success came some way after the Globe, but its distinctive shape towers in front of it. The Blackfriars was the heavy tree under whose shadow the Globe first struggled to grow.

## 3. THE MODERNIZED GLOBE

Up the stairs at the end of the exhibition's main story is the piazza with its view across the river to St Paul's, and on it the Globe. The Globe was built as a playhouse and has been reconstructed as a playhouse, and the ultimate prize of a visit to the complex is the performance of a play there. Through most of each day, though, the playhouse will be open for inspection as the crowning feature of the exhibition. It may have students rehearsing in it, or it may be free for visitors to try their own speeches in it. It may stand empty and open for completely free inspection. Empty playhouses can sometimes offer more than playhouses packed for a performance.

The rebuilt Globe will not attempt to disguise the changes which have been made from the original structure. Because it is intended for use as a performing theatre, for instance, it has to conform to modern fire regulations. A look at the ground plan will show that additional exits have been provided at ground level, and emergency stairways from the galleries. Conforming to the fire regulations is essential if the Globe is to be licensed as a theatre in the twentieth century. Since theatres only come to life through performance, these modifications to the original design were the inescapable price of making an exhibition which could live and work as Shakespeare's playhouse lived and worked. The modifications have been made openly and honestly. A note about the alterations we have been forced to make to the original design, and the principles according to which they were organized, is necessary here.

In 1622 John Fletcher, who collaborated with Shakespeare in writing several plays, and who followed him as resident playwright for the King's Men, wrote a play called *The Sea Voyage*. It deliberately imitated *The Tempest*, opening with a storm at sea and a shipwreck, and later showing the castaways at a banquet. One of the delicacies offered to the feasting castaways was potatoes. This was the first acknowledgement made by any dramatist of the existence of this now standard addition to Europe's appetite. In the twentieth century potatoes have added their bit to one of the more unanswerable difficulties involved in presenting the Globe of Shakespeare's time to modern visitors.

Since 1622 potatoes and all the other discoveries which have extended and improved the scope of humanity's food consumption have had their effect on human physique. The average size of a twentieth-century visitor to the Globe is almost ten per cent greater than the playgoer of Shakespeare's own time. The difference presented the designers of the Globe reconstruction with an awkward dilemma. If the original dimensions of the Globe were to be retained, modern visitors would experience it as a structure one-tenth smaller than they would have found it if they had seen it in 1600. The surrounding galleries would seem that bit more cramped. The players on the stage platform would appear that much larger than life, at least life as Shakespeare and his fellow-sharers conceived it in 1599. The space available for sitting on the 'degrees' or gallery benches would be that much smaller. The audience's sense of the acting space would be falsified. But then, if the designers chose the alternative course and enlarged every dimension by ten per cent, the result would be a distortion of the original in other ways. It could be argued that the smaller size is a useful reminder to the modern visitor that modern people are not and can never be Elizabethans, and on such a visit they have to piece out all the imperfections with their thoughts.

Neither of these alternatives offers a perfect solution. Either carries with it a chain of consequences which necessarily affect the final design in quite fundamental ways. A Globe built to the enlarged dimensions, for instance, would more easily accommodate the extra exits and other modern features which the fire regulations insist on. It would then be unequivocally a 'modernized' Globe. As such it would logically also be easy to provide it with modern lighting so that it would become available for use after dark, as a regular evening theatre. The trouble with such a design, though, is at least in part that there is no obvious point at which to stop the slide into modernization. Before long there would be a cry to create other modern conveniences such as a transparent roof against the weather, and the original conditions, and certainly the original acoustics, would be gone forever. The line where the authentic reconstruction of the original ends and modernization begins would be impossibly blurred, and the whole principle of authenticity would be lost. The Globe project was not conceived to create just another modern theatre, as a rival to the National Theatre or the Royal Shakespeare Company.

The other alternative, reproducing the original shape and the original dimensions as precisely as possible throughout, not only strengthens the principle of accurate historical reconstruction, but in most respects it makes the whole thing more consistent. With no more modernizing than the fire regulations demand, the original conditions for performance – daylight, open-air acoustics, the noise of a crowd on its feet, the intimate audience – will generate something more like the original Shakespeare in performance which is the ultimate goal for all these experiments. There are almost certainly other factors that we can only dimly perceive until we have reconstructed the original conditions of performance. Any compromise in the direction of modernization, any compromise which is not absolutely necessary for safety, must be rejected if the goal of getting to know Shakespeare's plays better is to be attainable.

That being said, let us look at the compromises which are necessary. In Chapter Three some of the changes made in the interests of safety from fire have been described. Using tiles instead of thatch on the gallery roofing is the first. Given the disaster that happened to the original Globe in 1613, and also given that originally the builders probably only used thatch as an economy measure because the financiers were short of cash, it makes sense. It is to some extent a painful choice to have to make, because it gives the Globe's exterior a look more like that of its replacement, the second Globe of 1614, than the original. We did in fact try various materials which might look more like thatch than black tiles do, including an artificial form of thatch used by some breweries when they want to offer a version of Ye Olde Englysshe Pubbe. Unfortunately the plastic variety of thatch also burned, and gave off such toxic fumes that it was even more dangerous than natural thatch. We have made sure that the Globe's tiles are black, which is roughly the colour of reasonably aged thatch, so that they will at least form a contrast with the red tiles of the surrounding roofs. The superstructure over the stage also differs from the original Globe in having tiles rather than thatch, like the gallery roof. This, it is well worth noting, has one distinct advantage for the spectator who chooses to stand in the yard to watch a play. Thatch allows water to run off straight from its eaves to the ground. Tiles on the other hand can have gutters, to carry rainwater out of harm's way. The Globe's tiles will save the spectators standing next to the stage under the rim of the stage cover from receiving any of the drips of water that a thatched roof would certainly deposit on them.

Otherwise the modernizations have been made conspicuous, to emphasize that they do not belong to the original design. Electrical fittings for the Exit signs will not be concealed, and the emergency lighting system will be an obviously modern addition. By far the largest modification introduced in the interests of safety is the increase in the number and size of the entries and exits, and the stairways. The enlargement of the stair turrets is one of the less obvious moderniz-ations, but the enlargement is not substantial, and the basic shape of the turrets is consistent with the evidence for the original shape. The four ground-floor exits from the yard, and their stairways to the galleries, are all modern additions, as are the gallery stairways alongside the tiring-house area. The broken line of the circuit of galleries around the yard at ground level is the clearest evidence on view for the inescapable modernizations which have been made to the original design. Ironically, it brings the design closer in appearance to the sketch Johannes de Witt made of the Swan in 1596, where the access to the galleries appears to be by stairways leading up from the yard, not from stair turrets. All these modifications, in any case, are at the outer edges of the auditorium, and have no effect on the viewing places in the auditorium itself, or on the stage area.

The most profound change required by the fire regulations is the maximum number of visitors allowed to crowd into the Globe at one time. The figure for the capacity of the original Globe, 3000 people, is neatly halved. Altogether about 1500 visitors will be able to squeeze into the galleries and yard of the reconstructed Globe to watch a performance. This halving of the capacity is an advantage in two ways. First, it means that people with modern physiques need not bother to undertake the painful labour of trying to fit themselves into the original 18-inch space allocated for Elizabethans. Secondly, the doubling of the available space makes it easy to conceive how squeezed Elizabethans were when the Globe was crowded. Also it is to be hoped that, when adjusting to the scale of the original auditorium and the crowds squeezing into its various spaces, modern spectators will find it easier to imagine two people standing or sitting in the space for one than they would to calculate 10 per cent or similar small fractions greater or less than the actual size. And of course in an enclosed space which totals barely 100 feet in diameter, even the halved capacity must still leave the 1500 spectators feeling fairly intimately grouped together. The analogy cited in the introductory chapter, of the playhouse crowd with a crowd at a football match, will not quite be lost.

Aside from these compulsory modernizations, the Globe will look much as it must have looked in Shakespeare's day. The exterior will be coated with lath, lime and hair, as specified in the builder's contract which Peter Street worked by at the Fortune, where he was enjoined to copy the Globe. The timbers in the interior will mostly be plastered and painted in the colours standard at the time. We cannot be sure of the acoustic effect of the Globe's peculiar combination of sounding-boards, plaster, woodwork and human bodies, and it is important to get that kind of detail right if the acoustic effects of speaking from the Globe's stage are to be assessed accurately. Some of the details are necessarily still highly conjectural. Even the tiring-house front at the rear of the stage platform is essentially a conjecture based on a minute scrutiny of the inadequate evidence that has survived. More obviously conjectural is the opening in the gable front over the stage where the trumpeter stands to advertise the start of a performance, and from which he runs up the Globe's flag. We know from de Witt's drawing of the Swan that the amphitheatres had such features, but we have no hard evidence about how the Globe's structure was arranged to provide for them. Given our conclusion about the gable-fronted construction over the stage, which was clearly a different kind of design from that of the Swan, it seemed most sensible to locate the trumpeter's platform in the gable, rather than to invent another opening close to the gallery ridge, as it is depicted at the Swan.

Inside the Globe other factors which at present are still unclear will obviously have something to add to the way audiences respond during a performance. The plain daylight will affect audiences as much as actors. Without any artificial light to blank out the spectators and focus attention on the stage, and with no spotlights to fix on individual actors, eyes will rove much more freely. Spectators might well find other spectators more interesting or attractive than the actors. The actors will have to respond to this challenge by greater emphasis either of action or personality, and certainly by more direct address to the audience, visible as it will be at the actors' feet. They will have to walk and talk through whatever the London weather may choose to throw at them. And, perhaps the greatest challenge of all, they will have to cope with the very special problems of outdoor acoustics.

Performing Shakespeare out of doors is in itself hardly a novelty. Performing the plays in a tightly constructed amphitheatre with walls 36 feet high all around, and a mass of mobile spectators damping most of the acoustic resonances from wall and fixed structures and generating noise of their own, certainly is new. Performances in open spaces like Regent's Park present problems to the actor of a completely different kind from the distinctive and quite unique challenges posed by the Globe. In central London too there is always likely to be a background of noise which will enter the amphitheatre quite as easily as the playing noises will escape it. In the early 1980s when the site for the project was first negotiated, there was a helicopter landing-pad on a barge anchored on the opposite side of the Thames from the project's site. The landing-pad was illegal, but it did a lot of business there for several years, and so long as it was there every take-off and every landing flooded the area with its noise. Helicopters produce sounds which are difficult to muffle at the best of times. If they are poised in mid-air a hundred feet above the open yard of the Globe even the loudest-voiced of actors would have difficulty making himself heard. It is to be hoped that the law banning helicopters, which is now restored, will remain unbroken for the lifetime of the Globe on Bankside. Other forms of London traffic on the whole are unlikely to be quite so obtrusive. The most obtrusive outdoor distraction will probably come from such locally-generated trifles as the noise of shuffling feet among the standers in the yard.

## 4. THE INIGO JONES PLAYHOUSE

By the 1630s the Blackfriars hall playhouse was overshadowing the Globe. The story of the hall playhouses is told chiefly by means of the Inigo Jones playhouse, the closest imitator of Shakespeare's Blackfriars playhouse and its closest rival in the later years of the Shakespearean period.

The Inigo Jones playhouse poses quite as many problems as the Globe. As a roofed theatre which originally had artificial lighting, it is an important performance space for use in the evenings. And so it too has to be subjected to the constraints of fire regulations. The lintels of its doors were originally designed by Jones at no more than five feet six inches high, a height difficult enough for the gallants wearing their ostrich-plumed hats, and quite insufficient to satisfy the regulations protecting modern playgoers. A mass panic exit through doors with lintels no higher than a modern nose or chin would cause a lot of pain as well as confusion, and endanger everyone. The doors have therefore been redesigned with a more manageable lintel height. It is worth noting here, perhaps, that in the entire seventy-five years up to 1642 when the public playhouses were operating in London, only two ever caught fire. In neither case was there any loss of life. With ten amphitheatres and six hall playhouses in more or less daily use, the burning of the Globe amphitheatre in 1613 and the Fortune amphitheatre in 1622 were the casualties in what must be judged a remarkably good safety record. That is not, of course, any justification for not making the modern reconstructions safe by modern standards.

The question of seating capacity is another acute problem under the pressure of the fire regulations. At the Globe the 1500 capacity can be made up partly from the open-space provision of the yard. There is less flexibility in an all-seat auditorium. At the smaller hall playhouse, by the same rules which applied to the Globe, many fewer spectators can now be positioned on the benches than the original capacity of six or seven hundred. The London Fire Brigade's licence permitting the use of the Inigo Jones theatre for public shows of any kind has in fact been generous, and allows about 330 spectators in all. This, rather remarkably, allows us to repeat the system used for the Globe, since it offers seating for about half the original capacity. In both theatres modern spectators can comfort themselves with the thought that they are occupying exactly twice the space they would have had in Shakespeare's time, whether they are 10 per cent larger than the Elizabethan average or not.

In all dimensions but one the stage area and the colonnades and gallery structure of the Inigo Jones theatre are precisely the size which

Jones laid down in his plans. The exception is the height from the stage level to the gallery behind the stage, which has been increased from 10 feet 6 inches to 11 feet, to give adequate headroom for modern figures. The scale of the auditorium itself, however, has in one respect had to be increased by the familiar 10 per cent. This is not done just because modern figures are that much larger than Elizabethan figures, but simply to improve the space behind the galleries for spectator access. On the same principle by which the stairways at the Globe had to be enlarged to allow for emergency exits, so the outer shell of the Inigo Jones theatre behind the galleries has been slightly expanded to create a more spacious walkway. The alteration is, like most of the changes at the Globe, confined to the back of the auditorium, and will not affect the forward view of the audience, nor the dimensions of the stage area.

Seating at the Inigo Jones theatre was originally made up of benches in the pit, and 'degrees' or broad planking like steps in the galleries and boxes. The degrees were in fact used as steps to provide access from behind. These degrees have been retained in the reconstruction, though on 50 per cent of them only feet will be planted, instead of bottoms and feet together. Some sections which in the original were part of the complete circuit of seating will remain as steps, and be kept clear to serve as aisles for the audience to come and go.

The only slightly odd and awkward feature of the auditorium as Jones designed it is the disposition of the benches in the pit. In his drawings the benches follow the curve of the galleries around a circuit with its pivot at the centre of the stage front. Thus people sitting at the edges of the benches nearest the stage will have to turn through 90 degrees to see the stage in front of them. The spectators just behind them will then have to peer over the shoulders of the people in the front seats, while at the same time looking awkwardly sideways in order to see the stage. It seems more logical as well as more comfortable to arrange the pit's benches in straight lines facing the stage, as they would be in a modern cinema. This presents our modern designers with a peculiar dilemma. Either we adopt the Jones scheme on the principle that we must assume he knew what he was doing, and that our object is to reproduce as precisely as we can the exact structure that he had in mind, or we introduce improvements of our own, presumably arguing that he would have designed them our way if he had realized what he was doing wrong. The latter is a very shaky kind of argument to maintain when the guiding principle for the entire project is to reconstruct the original designs in authentic detail so far as they can be rediscovered. The choice we have to make is, perhaps regrettably, obvious. Sitting with twisted necks on the curved benches in the Inigo Jones pit, we can at least console ourselves by acknowledging that the choice has the virtue of consistency.

The most distinctive single feature of the hall playhouses, apart from the comfort of shelter from the weather, was the lighting. There were windows which usually brought in some light from the afternoon sun (Thomas Dekker makes a comment which implies that when a gloomy tragedy was to be performed the boy companies closed the windows to make the atmosphere even darker). Generally, though, the main illumination, brightening the stage and the auditorium alike, came from large candelabra. The accounts for the Cockpit at Court in Whitehall suggest that as many as 150 candles were needed to illuminate a small hall playhouse. At the reconstructed Inigo Jones Cockpit candelabra will provide the main lighting. They will not, again because of the risk from fire, be the Elizabethan wax or rushlights: they will be electric (with flicker effect), with the candlepower of the 150 candles specified for the Court playhouse.

Thanks to the unique gift of his designs which Inigo Jones left to us, the reconstruction of his playhouse leaves room for much less guesswork and conjecture than its larger neighbour. Because of that, and because it is a smaller playhouse, there is even less room here for adaptation to suit modern requirements than at the Globe. It has a roof, and the electrical equivalent of candlelight, both of which will make it easier to use at night instead of in the afternoons when most Londoners (unlike their Elizabethan equivalents) are occupied at their work. It also has the peculiar distinction, if the design Jones produced was indeed used by Christopher Beeston for his Cockpit playhouse in 1616, of forming a bridge from the Shakespearean period of theatre design to the Restoration and modern period.

The Inigo Jones playhouse is a wonderful bonus for the project to reconstruct the Globe. As little as ten years ago it could not have been thought of as a significant contribution to the whole scheme. Now it supplies many needs – an absolutely authentic original design, a close neighbour and rival to the Blackfriars, an indoor playhouse, a bridge between Shakespearean and modern theatre designs – and this whole exhibition of the theatre world in and for which Shakespeare worked would be much less colourful and comprehensive without it. The location of this second reconstruction, poised for discovery after the experience of the Globe, should be as much of a delight as a surprise. Set as it is in a siding off the main lobby and reception area, quite possibly the hurried visitor might miss it altogether. That would be a major mistake. Its colour, its intimacy, its sometimes uncomfortable reality, the atmosphere of the first theatre ever to be built in Drury Lane–all make it the properly grand finale to the rediscovery of Shakespearean theatre which the whole exhibition makes possible.

Most museums contain skeletons, the residual but tangible remains of once living bodies. The Globe project has no skeletons. It is not a museum. The tangible relics of the playhouses of four centuries ago, the physical structures including the rebuilt playhouses themselves, supply no more than a framework for a display which we hope will continue in existence as a living body. The playhouse replicas and the exhibition are the basis for Shakespeare in the theatre, a living entity. The life of this new entity will not be just a matter of resurrecting old bones but of the excitement of modern discovery, a new life for old plays. It is of course possible that if we offer only a slavish obedience to what we think were the authentic Shakespearean originals we might produce no more than a kind of zombiedom, a living corpse. That would be, in one sense or another, as fatal as it would be if we offered the playhouses empty. The project is an experiment designed to produce life much more handsome than Frankenstein's monster. Shakespeare in performance, in a replica of his original working conditions: a complete novelty, and more than a novelty, a novel experiment. The experiment is aimed at retrieving some of the vital features of the essential Shakespeare, features of the plays which have been out of sight for the last four centuries. If it works, we shall have rediscovered some of the finest artefacts England has ever produced.

[171]

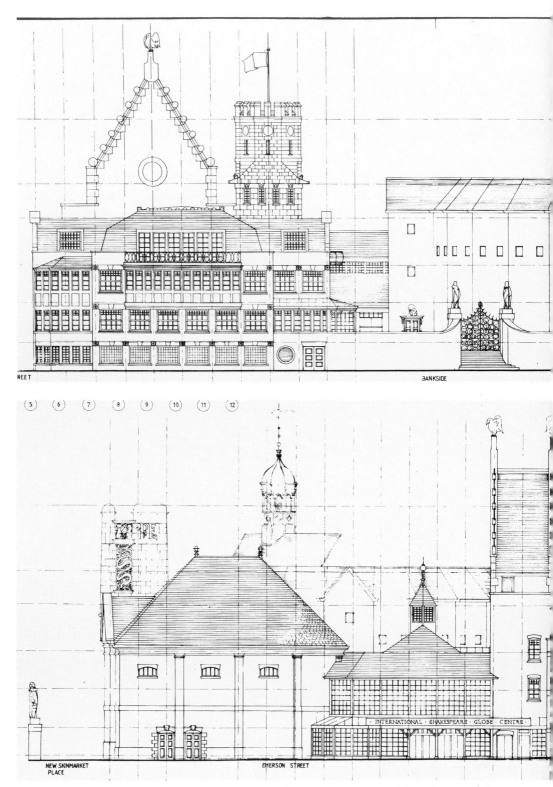

REET

BANKSIDE

⑤　⑥　⑦　⑧　⑨　⑩　⑪　⑫

INTERNATIONAL · SHAKESPEARE · GLOBE · CENTRE

NEW SKINMARKET
PLACE

EMERSON STREET

*44: Elevations of the new Globe complex from the north (top) and from the east, and a cross-section showing the tiring-house behind the stage, the stage and the galleries.*

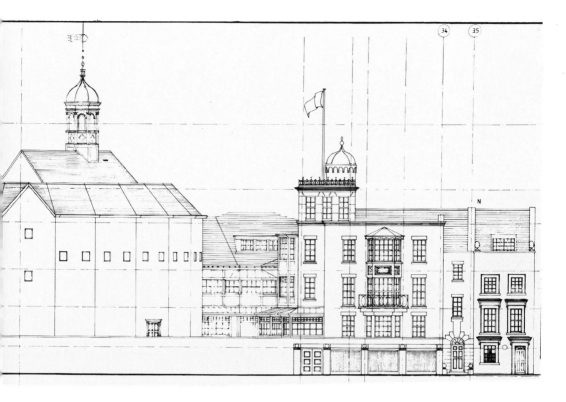

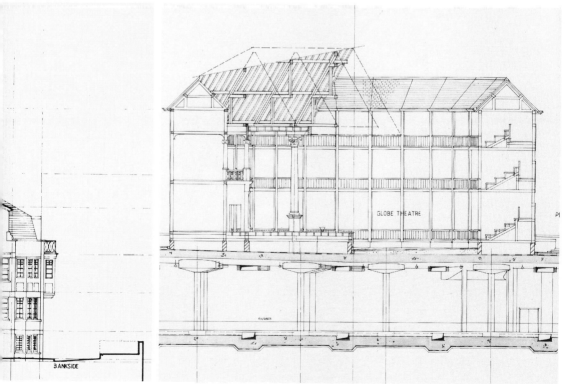

GLOBE THEATRE

BANKSIDE

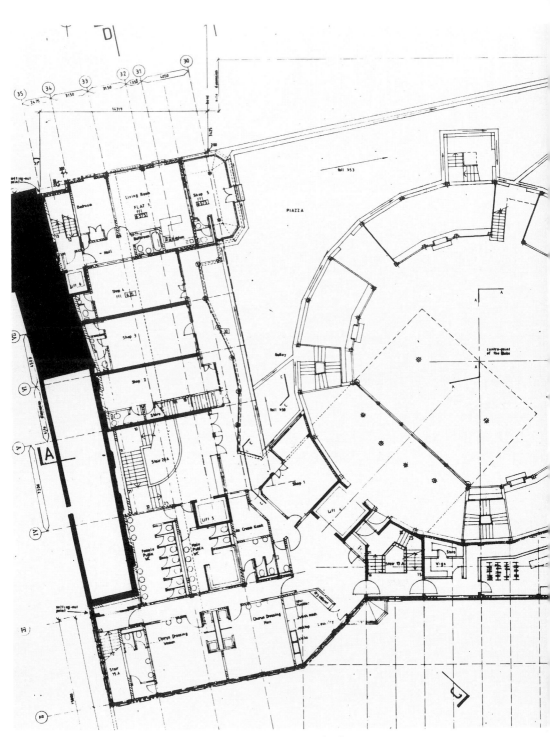

45: *Plan of the whole ISGC complex at piazza level.*
*The Inigo Jones theatre is at lower right.*

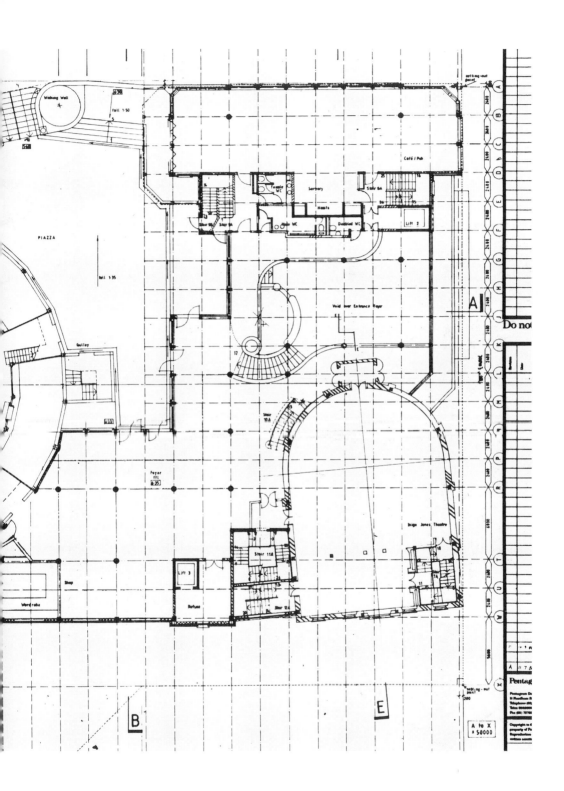

PIAZZA

Wishing Well

fall 1:50

fall 1:35

Gulley

Café / Pub

Female WC

Servery

Stair 8A

Male WC

Dibbled WC

Heals

LIFT 2

Stair 8B

Stair 8A

Void over Entrance Foyer

Stair 10A

Foyer FFL

Inigo Jones Theatre

Stair 11A

Stair 12A

Lift 3

Wardrobe

Shop

Refuse

A

B

E

Pentagram

A to X = 50000

Do not

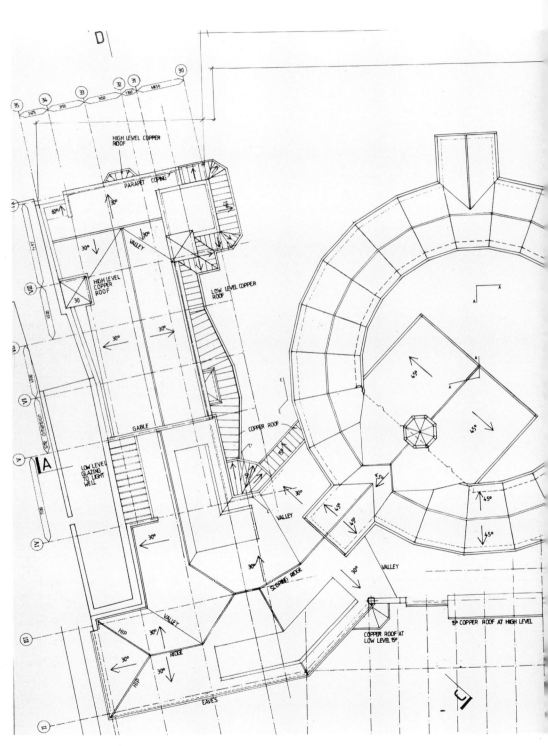

46: *Roof plan of the complex.*

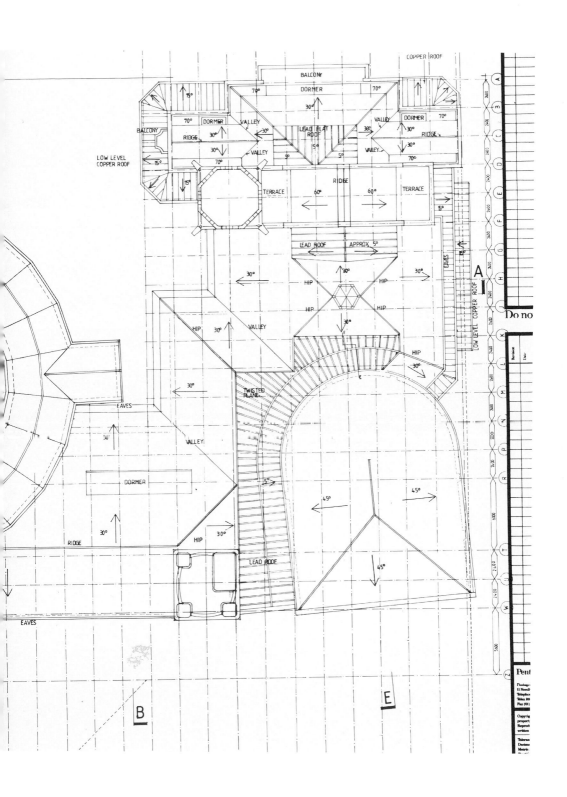

*Paul Cox's colour illustrations re-create the Globe and Inigo Jones theatres as they might have appeared in 1599 and 1616.*

# NOTES ON THE COLOUR ILLUSTRATIONS

**I. The Globe as it might have been in 1599. A bird's-eye view looking east towards London Bridge and the Tower.**

This artist's impression uses the evidence about the buildings of Shakespeare's time shown in Hollar's 'Long View' and Norden's *Civitas Londini*, in order to represent the Globe from an imaginary perspective just above it and a little to the west. It looks past the Globe to London Bridge. Beyond it on the skyline you can see the four turrets of the Tower of London, while at the southern end of the bridge stands the tower of Saint Mary Overies (Southwark Cathedral) from which Norden and Hollar drew their panoramas. The different forms of transport available to playgoers are all shown here. Wherries on the river are making their way to the Bankside landing. A lady is getting down from her coach, which stands by one of the two stair turrets forming the main entrance-ways to the playhouse. Among the pedestrians stand some horses (popular legend said that Shakespeare started his playhouse career by holding horses at the door). In the crowd you can see beggars, a performing bear, and vendors selling different kinds of produce.

On a summer afternoon in 1599, at two o'clock (GMT), the sun shines on the thatched roof of the Globe, which is already packed with playgoers waiting for the performance to start. The start is being signalled by the flag and the busy trumpeter. On the flag you can just make out the figure of Hercules and his load, the Globe's emblem which is joked about in *Hamlet*. Out of sight behind the playhouse is the tavern which the Burbages leased along with the site. It probably supplied the vendors who squeezed through the playhouse crowd selling their bottled beer or water and various foodstuffs.

[179]

**II. The Globe as it might have been in 1599. A view of the stage from the yard.**

The viewpoint here is that of a playgoer paying only the minimal one-penny admission for standing room in the playhouse yard. He (it was mostly apprentices, male house-servants and handcraft artisans who made up the 'understanders' in the yard) is surrounded by people wearing the flat caps of artisans, while the middle-class citizen-employers and their wives in the galleries wear higher-crowned hats, and the nobles in the lords' rooms over the stage are crowned with feathers. In the galleries citizen blue mixes with the scarlet of the nobility. Few of the standers could afford the luxury of smoking, which was usually a pastime in the lords' rooms. It is a sunny afternoon, and the standers need not fear the dripping of water from the eaves on each side of the stage cover, which would have continued to shed water for days after a downpour. In the yard on the left and the right can be seen vendors of fruit and drink, while behind one artisan a young cutpurse is snipping some profit for himself. The stage itself towers over the understanders, its 'shadow' or 'heavens' showing itself to be 'fretted with gold fire' as Hamlet describes it. On stage we see a scene which might be from *Titus Andronicus*. The Roman emperor on his throne wears a toga while Tamora on her (his) knees begs for her sons' lives. For all the Roman setting of the play, the Roman soldiers on either side by the stage pillars wear the standard garb of the Elizabethan soldiery, as they do in Henry Peacham's drawing of a similar scene from the play.

**III. The Globe as it might have been in 1599. A view of the stage from the top gallery.**

This view is from a twopenny gallery at the highest level, looking down on the Globe's stage. The people here are gentry and citizens, perhaps army captains on leave from the wars in the Netherlands, sea captains, lawyers, and idle men about town who lack the money or the self-possession to display themselves in the more expensive and conspicuous seats. They sit on the wooden benches or 'degrees' which rise steeply from the gallery rail. These 'degrees' form the stairs which give access from the rear corridor as well as providing the seating for the galleries. There are ladies and citizens' wives here, each accompanied by a male escort to make it clear that they are not whores or 'game' for sexual adventures.

They look down on a scene at a royal court, where the king sits on his throne, sceptre in hand, listening to a bare-headed pleader. There is war in the air, signalled by the banners on stage and the attendant's drum. A new character is about to enter at stage left, by the right-hand entry door. Above the stage in the 'heavens' can be seen a small cannon, the kind of 'chamber' which was fired in battle scenes such as the one at Harfleur in *Henry V*, and for special ceremonials such as in *Hamlet*, when Claudius orders the trumpet to signal to the cannon and the cannon to fire every time he drinks. This was the cannon which, in 1613 at a performance of *Henry VIII*, shot a piece of wadding into the thatch over the galleries, and started the fire which burned the first Globe to the ground.

[181]

**IV. The Inigo Jones theatre as it might have been in 1616.**

A view from the lower of the two galleries at the hall playhouse designed by Inigo Jones. The brightly coloured hall, with its glittering candelabra, creates a much more intimate atmosphere here than the Globe's amphitheatre. The audience is more exclusively gentlemanly and noble than at the Globe. Lace and rich brocade are more visible in this audience, and there are fewer citizens. In the pit at this playhouse, unlike in the yard at the Globe, they all sit on benches, though in the galleries they sit on the same kind of wooden 'degrees' as at the Globe. The audience still surrounds the players just as it does at the Globe, sitting in boxes on each side of the stage and in the balcony above the stage doors. The most obtrusive gallants sit on stools on the stage itself, in front of the boxes.

Unlike the Globe's great platform stage, this stage has a rail cutting the players off from the audience in the pit. The origins of the kind of structure which would be turned into proscenium arch or 'picture-frame' stages in later theatres can be seen here. It is a much more intimate enclosed space than the open-air Globe, the design for theatres of the future. Like the Globe it is brightly painted, though with a special reason here for its lavish use of gilding. This had the effect of catching and reflecting the gleams of light from the candelabra which lit the theatre. The brightness of the decor matched the brilliance of the audience's dress, their jewels, pomanders, feathers and fans. The sixty or so flickering candles in the candelabra hanging from the ceiling and lodged in the sconces on the pillars were a more familiar kind of lighting to Elizabethan playgoers than to moderns accustomed to the steady glow of electric light. They dressed with a sparkle designed to catch the flickering candlelight.

But the play and the stage were the main focus. Behind the candles in their sconce on the left-hand pillar you can see the shape of the curtained music room over the stage. From here came the concert which formed an overture to the performance, and the music which accompanied the songs in the play. The actors are playing a scene like the one shown in the vignette from *Roxana*.

# NOTES

## CHAPTER ONE

1. The story of the dispute is told in E. K. Chambers, *The Elizabethan Stage*, 4 vols. Oxford University Press, Oxford, 1923. II.398–400. See also Andrew Gurr, 'Money or Audiences: the Impact of Shakespeare's Globe', *Theatre Notebook* 42 (1988), pp. 3–14.

2. See *The Elizabethan Stage*, II.203, 214.

3. Originally noted by Leslie Hotson in *Shakespeare's Wooden O*, Rupert Hart-Davies, London (1959), the point has been affirmed with precision by Alan R. Young. 'The Orientation of the Elizabethan Stage: "That Glory of the Sober West"', *Theatre Notebook* 33 (1979), pp. 80–85; and John Orrell, 'Sunlight at the Globe', *Theatre Notebook* 38 (1984), pp 69–76.

4. Richard Brome, *The Antipodes*, I.iv.

5. *Bartholomew Fair*, Induction.

6. Robert Speaight, *William Poel and the Elizabethan Revival*, William Heinemann, London, 1954, pp. 212–13.

7. W. W. Braines, *The Site of the Globe Playhouse, Southwark*, revised edn., London County Council, 1924.

8. *Saturday Review*, 5 November 1897, reprinted in *Our Theatres in the Nineties*, 3 vols, Constable, London, 1932, III.241–44.

9. *The Diary of John Manningham* ed. R. Parker Sorlien, University Press of New England, Hanover, NH, 1967, p. 48.

10. Edward Gordon Craig, *On the Art of the Theatre*, William Heinemann, London, 1911, pp. 289–92.

12. See Cary M. Mazer, *Shakespeare Refashioned: Elizabethan Plays on Edwardian Stages*, UMI Research Press, Ann Arbor, 1981, p. 75, and Harley Granville Barker, *The Exemplary Theatre*, Chatto and Windus, London, 1922. Barker's book states the case after ten years of campaigning by the Shakespeare National Theatre Committee.

13. A brochure, entitled 'The Age of Shakespeare Lives Again', was issued in 1935 by The Globe–Mermaid Association of England and America. Beautifully illustrated by F. C. Faery, its founder, F. C. Owlett, commissioned Kenneth Cross as the project architect. The Globe itself was to be twice the original size and roofed in glass.

14. I. A. Shapiro demolished the key piece of evidence on which Adams based his eight-sided reconstruction in 1948. See note 20. Shapiro also demolished the idea that Shakespeare was a regular at the Mermaid tavern celebrated in Beaumont's poem and a feature of the Globe–Mermaid project.

15. The Swan drawing is well known. It was discovered in Utrecht by the German scholar K. T. Gaedaertz. See Chapter Three, note 19.

16. Published in four volumes, in succession to the three of Chamber's *The Medieval Stage*, Chambers's volumes take the documentation up to 1616. G. E. Bentley extended the work to 1642 with another seven volumes, in *The Jacobean and Caroline Stage*, Oxford University Press, Oxford, 1941–68.

17. J. Cranford Adams, *The Globe Playhouse, its design and equipment*, Harvard University Press, Cambridge, Mass., 1942.

18. Irwin Smith, *Shakespeare's Globe Playhouse*, Peter Owen, London, 1956. Smith's book, which came out eight years after Shapiro's analysis had challenged the basis for Adams's and Smith's work, took little account of it. Smith's later book, *Shakespeare's Blackfriars Playhouse*, Peter Owen, London, 1964, is much more reliable.

19. *The Staging of Elizabethan Plays at the Red Bull Theatre*, Oxford University Press, London, 1940.

20. I. A. Shapiro, 'The Bankside Theatres: Early Engravings', *Shakespeare Survey* I (1948), pp. 25–37.

21. *The Quest for Shakespeare's Globe*, Cambridge University Press, Cambridge, 1983.

22. The findings of the last two seminars appeared as supplements to *Renaissance Drama Newsletter*, published by the University of Warwick. The first, 'The Shape of the Globe', appeared in 1983. The second, 'The Interior of the Globe', jointly with the reissued 'Shape' report, appeared in 1987.

23. See *The Elizabethan Stage*, IV. 319–20.

24. It has an act break, a practice peculiar to hall playhouses, between the end of Act IV and the beginning of Act V. Prospero and Ariel leave the stage to conclude Act IV, and re-enter to begin Act V.

25. See Richard Hosley, *The Revels History of Drama in English*, III (1576–1613), Methuen, London, 1976, pp. 197–226.

26. The nine amphitheatres were, in order of construction, the Red Lion (1567), the Theatre (1576), the Curtain (1577), the Rose (1587), the Swan (1595), the Globe (1599), the Fortune (1600), the Boar's Head (1601) and the Red Bull (1604). A tenth amphitheare, the Hope, was built in 1614 to serve a double function as a playhouse and bear-baiting house. Its career as the former was quickly absorbed by the latter. The hall playhouses were Paul's (1575), the first Blackfriars (1576), the second Blackfriars (1596, first performances 1600), the Cockpit (1616) and Salisbury Court (1629).

27. Don Rowan rediscovered the drawings in the library of Worcester College, Oxford, and wrote about them in 1969. Iain Mackintosh first suggested that they might have been drawn for Christopher Beeston's Cockpit in 1973, a view amplified and confirmed by John Orrell in 1977. Recently Graham Bradshaw has challenged this interpretation on the grounds that there was no plot of land in Drury Lane suitable for the building set out in the drawings. See Chapter 4, note 17.

28. See John Orrell, *The Theatres of Inigo Jones and John Webb*, Cambridge University Press, Cambridge, 1985, pp. 60–74.

29. See Chapter Four, p. 154.

# NOTES
## CHAPTER TWO

1. Thomas Platter, *Travels in England*, trans. Clare Williams, Jonathan Cape, London, 1951, pp. 166–67. The translation has been slightly adapted.

2. The evidence on which parts of this chapter have been based is presented at greater length in the author's *Playgoing in Shakespeare's London*, Cambridge University Press, Cambridge, 1987.

3. Sir John Davies, *Epigrammes* 17, 'In Cosmum', in *The Poems of Sir John Davies*, ed. Robert Krueger, Clarendon Press, Oxford, 1975, pp. 135–36.

4. *Pierce Penilesse*, 1592, F3r.

5. Anon, *A Warning for Fair Women*, 1599, line 75.

6. In a verse about an idle gallant, Sir John Davies wrote
   First he doth rise at 10 and at eleven
   He goes to Gyls where he doth eate till one,
   Then sees a play till sixe, and sups at seaven ...
   (*Epigrammes* 39, *The Poems* ed. Krueger, p. 146).

7. John Taylor, 'The True Cause of the Water-mens Suit concerning Players', 1614, in *Works*, 1630, p. 172.

8. Mildmay's records of his playgoing are summarized in G. E. Bentley, *The Jacobean and Caroline Stage*, II.673–81.

9. Quoted in *The Jacobean and Caroline Stage*, I. 4–5.

10. George Garrard, *Strafforde's Letters*, I. 175–76 (9 January 1634).

11. John Marston, *Jack Drum's Entertainment*, 1601, Act V.

12. *Travels in England*, p. 167.

13. Sir John Davies, *Epigrammes* 36, *The Poems*, ed. Krueger, p. 144.

14. Sir Thomas Overbury, *Characters*, ed. W. J. Paylor, Basil Blackwell, Oxford, 1936, p. 41.

15. I owe this observation to Colin Sorensen of the Museum of London.

16. *Travels in England*, p. 176.

17. The engraving is reproduced in the author's *Playgoing in Shakespeare's London*, p. 37.

18. Michael Drayton, Sonnet 47, 'Idea' in *Works*, ed. Hebel, 5 vols, Basil Blackwell, Oxford, 1932–41, II.334.

19. William Fennor, *Fennors Descriptions*, 1616, B2v.

20. Ben Jonson, *Every Man Out of his Humour*, in *Works*, ed. Herford and Simpson, 11 vols, Clarendon Press, Oxford, III.434.

21. John Marston, *What You Will*, 1601, Induction.

22. *The Gull's Hornbook*, 1610, Chapter 6.

23. John Marston, *The Scourge of Villainy*, 1598, G7v.

24. Sir John Harington, *Letters and Epigrams*, ed. N. E. McLure, University of Pennsylvania Press, Philadelphia, 1930, p. 31.

25. Scott McMillin, 'Simon Jewell and the Queen's Men', *Review of English Studies*, 27 (1976), pp. 174–77.

# NOTES

26. Samuel Schoenbaum, *William Shakespeare: A Compact Documentary Life*, Clarendon Press, Oxford, 1977, p. 234.

27. The main information about all of these players is given in E. K. Chambers, *The Elizabethan Stage*, II. 304–41.

28. Henslowe's 'Diary' was edited by R. A. Foakes and R. T. Rickert as *Henslowe's Diary*, Cambridge University Press, Cambridge, 1961. The Henslowe papers were edited in facsimile by R. A. Foakes, Scolar Press, London, 1977.

29. Schoenbaum, *William Shakespeare*, p. 207.

30. See for instance David Bevington, *Action is Eloquence: Shakespeare's Language of Gesture*, Harvard University Press, Cambridge, Mass., 1984; Alan C. Dessen, *Elizabethan Stage Conventions and Modern Interpreters*, Cambridge University Press, Cambridge, 1984; and the author's *The Shakespearean Stage, 1574–1642* second edition, Cambridge University Press, Cambridge, 1980.

31. John Davies of Hereford wrote an epigram addressed to Shakespeare in his *Scourge of Folly*, 1610, in which he says rather cryptically, 'Hadst thou not played some kingly parts in sport,/Thou hadst been a companion for a king.'

32. A thoroughly detailed but all too often unreliable study of possible 'lines' in Shakespeare's company is T. W. Baldwin's *The Organisation and Personnel of the Shakespearean Company*. Princeton University Press, Princeton, NJ, 1927.

33. The contract is in the Henslowe papers. It is reproduced in *The Shakespearean Stage, 1574–1642*, pp. 67–68.

34. *A Warning for Fair Women*, 1599, lines 82–83.

35. The vignette for *Messallina*, 1640. It is reproduced in *The Shakespearean Stage*, p. 139.

36. The anecdotes about Tarlton and Reade are printed in *The Shakespearean Stage*, pp. 86 and 92.

37. Sir Thomas Smith, *De Republica Anglorum*, Book II, Chapter 4.

38. Letter by Phillip Gawdy, quoted in *Playgoing in Shakespeare's London*, p. 57.

39. *The Jacobean and Caroline Stage*, II.361.

40. See *The Shakespearean Stage*, p. 194.

41. For a full examination of the use of funeral scenes on the Shakespearean stage, see Michael Neill's chapter in *Pageantry in the Shakespearean Theater*, ed. David Bergeron, University of Georgia Press, Athens, Ga, 1985, pp. 153–93.

42. See Richard Hosley, 'Was there a Music-Room in Shakespeare's Globe?' *Shakespeare Survey* 13 (1960), pp. 113–23.

43. For a more detailed survey of this matter see *Playgoing in Shakespeare's London*, Chapter 5, section f. 'Current Affairs'.

44. Thomas Nashe, *Pierce Penilesse*, 1592, F3v.

45. The letter was originally transcribed and translated by Geoffrey Tillotson, *Times Literary Supplement*, 20 July 1933, p. 494. The translation given here has been adapted slightly.

## NOTES

## CHAPTER THREE

1. The contemporary accounts of the Globe's burning are printed in E. K. Chambers, *The Elizabethan Stage*, II.419–23.

2. *Ibid.*, II.419 and 423.

3. *Ibid.*, II.426.

4. Herbert Berry, *Shakespeare's Playhouses*, AMS Press, New York, 1987, p. 235.

5. The theatre is partly described in a covenant recently discovered and published by Janet Loengard, 'An Elizabethan Lawsuit: John Brayne, his Carpenter, and the Building of the Red Lion Theatre,' *Shakespeare Quarterly* 34 (1983), pp. 298–310.

6. The documents were first printed by C. W. Wallace. They are reprinted in Herbert
  Berry, *Shakespeare's Playhouses*, Chapters 3 and 4.

7. *Ibid.*, p. 6.

8. The terms are reviewed by Chambers, *The Elizabethan Stage*, II.416–17.

9. Leslie Hotson, *Shakespeare's Wooden O*, pp. 264–69; C. J. Sisson, *The Boar's Head Theatre*, ed. Stanley Wells, Routledge and Kegan Paul, London, 1972; and Herbert Berry, *The Boar's Head Playhouse*, Folger Books, Washington DC, 1986.

10. Norden's panorama, the *Civitas Londini* (1600), is discussed by R. A. Foakes, *Illustrations of the English Stage 1580–1642*, Scolar Press, London, 1985, pp. 10–13.

11. For Hondius and Delaram see *ibid.*, pp. 14–17.

12. For Visscher see *ibid.*, pp. 18–19.

13. In 1924 W. W. Braines pointed out that Visscher seemed to have based his Bankside on the so-called 'Agas' map, which also derived from lost copperplate original: *The Site of the Globe Playhouse, Southwark*, pp. 51–53. Parts of the copperplate map have been discovered since Braines first posited its existence (p. 48). Nevertheless a detailed comparison shows that Visscher's source was not the 'Agas' map but the London map contained in the *Civitates Orbis Terrarum*, by G. Braun and F. Hogenberg (Cologne, 1572).

14. 'The Bankside Theatres: Early Engravings', *Shakespeare Survey I* (1948), pp. 27–28 and 30.

15. Underneath the eaves at the Swan Norden shows what might be intended as rows of tiny windows; Visscher interprets these as a decorative corbel table, and repeats them at the Beargarden and the Globe.

16. See Adams, *The Globe Playhouse*, pp. 24–26.

17. For the engraving see Foakes, *Illustrations of the English Stage*, pp. 8–9. The identification of the Theatre was first made by Sidney Fisher, *The Theatre, the Curtain and the Globe*, McGill University Library, Montreal, 1964.

18. For the two Hollar drawings see Foakes, *Illustrations of the English Stage*, pp. 29–31.

19. For the de Witt sketch see *ibid.*, pp. 52–55; de Witt's narrative is printed in Chambers, *The Elizabethan Stage*, II.361–63.

20. The Hope contract is printed in ibid., II.466–67.

21. The Fortune contract is printed in *Henslowe's Diary*, pp. 306–10.

22. See John Orrell, *The Quest for Shakespeare's Globe*, pp. 108–17.

23. *Ibid.*, pp. 16–31.

24. See Foakes, *Illustrations of the English Stage*, pp. 24–25.

25. See Sydney Anglo, *Spectacle, Pageantry and Early Tudor Policy*, Clarendon Press, Oxford, 1969, p. 159.

26. In 'Decorative and Mechanical Effect Relevant to the Theatre of Shakespeare,' in *The Third Globe*, edited by C. Walter Hodges and others, Wayne State University Press, Detroit, 1981, p. 190.

27. Cited by Chambers, *The Elizabethan Stage*, II.442.

28. *Henslowe's Diary*, p. 7.

29. 'Peep through thy marble mansion'; 'The marble pavement closes; he is entered/ His radiant roof.' So Sicilius observes the descent and ascent of Jupiter (*Cymbeline* V, v, 181 and 214–15).

30. Peter Street was responsible for 'seelinge' 'the gentlemens roomes Twoe pennie roomes and Stadge' at the Fortune. See *Henslowe's Diary*, p. 308.

31. 'This most excellent canopy the air, look you, this brave o'erhanging, this majestical roof fretted with golden fire . . .' *Hamlet* II. ii, 300–02.

32. See Margaret Jourdain, *English Decorative Plasterwork of the Renaissance*, Batsford, London, 1927, pp. 25–29; and Lawrence A. Turner, 'A Middlesex Jacobean Plasterer', *Country Life* 35 (1914), pp. 919–22.

33. See for example Richard Hosley, 'The Swan Playhouse (1595)', in *The Revels History of Drama in English*, III.164–72.

34. See the drawings by C. Walter Hodges in Berry, *The Boar's Head Playhouse*, pp. 146, 148 and 153–55.

35. A notable exception is Glynne Wickham, *Early English Stages 1300–1660*, 4 vols, Routledge and Kegan Paul, London, 1959–, II (part 1), 300–06.

36. *Troilus and Cressida* I, iii, 155–56.

37. *The Quest for Shakespeare's Globe*, pp. 153–55.

38. An account of this experiment is given in my article 'Sunlight at the Globe', *Theatre Notebook* 38 (1984), pp. 69–76 and plates 1–4.

# CHAPTER FOUR

1. For the Durham House view see *The Quest for Shakespeare's Globe*, pp. 18–19. The post-Fire view is Wenceslas Hollar, 'A True and Exact Prospect of the Famous City of London'.

2. 'The Second Blackfriars Playhouse (1596)', in *The Revels History of Drama in English*, III.202–03.

3. The terms of the indenture are given in Irwin Smith, *Shakespeare's Blackfriars Playhouse*, pp. 471–75. The Epilogue to Davenant's *Love and Honour*, performed 'at the Black-Fryers' in 1634, gives a touching picture of the audience using these stairs:

> Our Poet waits below to heare his destiny;
> Just in the Entry as you passe, the place
> Where first you mention your dislike or grace:

Pray whisper softly that he may not heare,
Or else such words as shall not blast his eare.

(1649 edn., p. 35)

4. PRO C115/M35/8391, cited by Bentley, *The Jacobean and Caroline Stage*, VI.6.

5. See the drawing by J. H. Farrar, based on the research by G. Topham Forrest, in *The Times*, 21 November 1921, p. 5; Smith, *Shakespeare's Blackfriars Playhouse*, pp. 290–94; and Hosley, *The Revels History of Drama in English*, III.211–12.

6. 1640 edn., sig. A3.

7. *The Witts* (1636), 'The Prologue, spoken at the Black Fryars'.

8. 'A Neglected Jones/Webb Theatre Project: "Barber-Surgeons' Hall Writ Large"', *New Theatre Magazine* 9 no. 3 (1969), pp. 6–15; also in *Shakespeare Survey* 23, (1970), pp. 125–29.

9. The evidence is slight, but is well reviewed by Smith, *Shakespeare's Blackfriars Playhouse*, pp. 290–92.

10. The Swan drawing, the vignettes and title pages are all discussed in Foakes, *Illustrations of the English Stage*, pp. 52–55, 72–73, 80–81 and 159–61.

11. See Rudolf Wittkower, 'The Renaissance Baluster and Palladio', in *Palladio and English Palladianism*, Thames and Hudson, London, 1974, pp. 41–48.

12. See, for example, the disguising house at Greenwich, 1527, described in Anglo, *Spectacle, Pageantry and Early Tudor Policy*, pp. 216–17.

13. Frontispiece designs survive for *The Shepherd's Paradise*, (1633) and *Florimene* (1635).

14. Wickham, *Early English Stages*, II (part 2). 144–47.

15. Rowan, 'A Neglected Jones/Webb Theatre Project', *Shakespeare Survey* 23, p. 127.

16. In John Harris, Stephen Orgel and Roy Strong, *The King's Arcadia: Inigo Jones and the Stuart Court*, Arts Council of Great Britain, London, 1973, p. 109.

17. *Records of the Honorable Society of Lincoln's Inn*, 5 vols, London 1897–1968, II.186, dated 15 October 1616. In his map-view of West London (*c.* 1657), Wenceslas Hollar shows the site of the Cockpit occupied by a three-bay house of two or three storeys. Such a structure could not have been used as an auditorium, whether a sporting cockpit or a playhouse, because its roof needed to be supported by load-bearing walls at each bay. Hollar's picture is probably an imaginary 'in-fill'. Nevertheless Graham F. Barlow, 'Wenceslas Hollar and Christopher Beeston's Phoenix Theatre in Drury Lane', *Theatre Research International* 13 (1988), pp. 30–44, argues from the evidence of deeds and leases concerning the site that Hollar's view is substantially correct. The deeds are, however, far from definitive in this matter, and Hollar is contradicted by William Morgan's generally accurate survey of 1681–82, which shows what then remained of the Cockpit as a rectangular block east of Drury Lane

18. T. J. King, 'The Staging of Plays at the Phoenix in Drury Lane, 1617–42', *Theatre Notebook*, 19 (1964–65), pp. 146–66.

19. *Malone Society Collections*, II (part 3). 382.

20. It is to this period, *c.* 1638–39, that Gordon Higgott has assigned Jones's drawings of the theatre itself. Higgott's dating, in an unpublished thesis for the University of London, is based on technical aspects of the draftsmanship, but ignores Rowan's evidence about the watermark. If it is correct it would appear that the drawings were connected with the regime of the King's and Queen's Boys at the Cockpit, the only

known royal initiative of the period likely to have involved the Surveyor in a theatrical enterprise. There being no evidence of extensive refitting of the Cockpit at this time, beyond the installation of scenery, the drawings would have been fine surveys intended for presentation, and Jones's role as the original designer would be in doubt.

21. Leslie Hotson, *The Commonwealth and Restoration Stage*, Harvard University Press, Cambridge, Mass., 1928, p. 96.

# INDEX